Solvency II

To Theresa, a brave and faithful heart

Solvency II

Stakeholder Communications and Change

Second Edition

GABRIELLE O'DONOVAN

Routledge
Taylor & Francis Group

LONDON AND NEW YORK

First published 2014 by Gower Publishing

Published 2016 by Routledge
2 Park Square, Milton Park, Abingdon, Oxon OX14 4RN
711 Third Avenue, New York, NY 10017, USA

Routledge is an imprint of the Taylor & Francis Group, an informa business

British Library Cataloguing in Publication Data
A catalogue record for this book is available from the British Library.

Library of Congress Cataloging-in-Publication Data
O'Donovan, Gabrielle.
 Solvency II : stakeholder communications and change / by Gabrielle O'Donovan.
  pages cm
 Revised edition of the author's Solvency II, published in 2011.
 Includes bibliographical references and index.
 ISBN 978-1-4724-4090-7 (paperback)
 1. Business communication. 2. Organizational change. I. Title.
 HF5718.O34 2014
 658.4'5–dc23

2014008411

ISBN 9781472440907 (pbk)

CONTENTS

LIST OF FIGURES

LIST OF TABLES

ABOUT THE AUTHOR

As a change management expert, Gabrielle O'Donovan has worked on a variety of large programmes to align the workforce and other stakeholders with business priorities. At Friends Life, Gabrielle led stakeholder management and communications for the Solvency II programme during Trevor Matthews' tenure as CEO. She had similar responsibilities at Dublin Airport Authority (DAA), Ireland, for the building of Terminal Two and was instrumental in helping the DAA achieve capital expenditure approval from the Regulator. Prior to that, Gabrielle led a multiple award-winning change management programme for HSBC bank, Hong Kong and five subsidiary companies. 'Together, We Win!' established a service culture in the bank which went on to win the Hong Kong industry 'Grand Award for Customer Service' for the first time in history. 'Together We Win!' also won an ASTD Excellence in Practice Award 2005 (USA), and a Best Practice in Training and Development Award 2003 (Hong Kong).

Gabrielle's first book, *The Corporate Culture Handbook*, was rated in the 'top 1 per cent of best business books for 2006' by lead USA reviewers *Business Book Review*. She is also author of a number of papers published in *Corporate Governance International*, *Banking Today*, *Best Practices Management* and the *International Journal of Knowledge, Culture and Change*. Gabrielle has lectured on culture and change as an Associate Professor for the MBA programme at Danube University, Krems, Austria, and for a master's degree module on organizational culture and change at Hong Kong Polytechnic University, China. She is a sought-after keynote speaker on the international circuit and is on the Advisory Board of Emerald Management First.

Gabrielle has a Master's Degree from the University of Sheffield, UK. She has numerous professional affiliations, including membership of the Association of Change Management Practitioners (APMG), and is a member of Mensa. Gabrielle lived in Hong Kong for 13 years, retaining strong connections with the region, and is now based in Richmond, Surrey, UK. She can be contacted at: director@gabrielleodonovan.com.

ABOUT THIS BOOK

With the Solvency II deadline approaching, and full implementation expected from January 2016, affected entities are at varying states of readiness, with embedding Solvency II into everyday practices becoming a major focus. Programme Stakeholder Communications need to be robust to secure compliance and buy-in on both internal and external fronts. If your CEO fails to communicate to the markets your organization's ability to deliver on the EU Directive, or if a local Regulator finds that your Board has failed to embed a risk culture that is aligned with Solvency II, your ability to operate in the Solvency II world will be questioned.

Solvency II: Stakeholder Communications and Change demonstrates how to negate such risks. It demonstrates how to establish, implement and maintain a stakeholder management and communications framework which supports people through change and which is framed by the European Union Solvency II Directive supporting guidance; in particular:

> *insurance and reinsurance undertakings shall have in place a system of governance which complies with at least, the following; to establish, implement and maintain effective cooperation, internal reporting and communication of information at all levels of the undertaking ...*

> *... insurance and reinsurance undertakings shall have in place an appropriate culture and environment that supports effective internal control activities, effective information and communication procedures and adequate monitoring mechanisms.*

Solvency II: Stakeholder Communications and Change also contains ground-breaking work on how to create a Solvency II compliant risk culture, using the 'risk culture framework' to embed desired values and behaviours. This approach provides optimal support for the Solvency II approval process and life in the Solvency II world. The focus of *Solvency II: Stakeholder Communications and Change* is, in essence, managing people through change in a regulatory change context.

This book is organized into eight chapters, each designed to share best practices and lessons learnt, using plain language, clear examples and providing new and practical tools and models. This book takes an industry-wide perspective and is based on a number of years' experience working in the programme management regulatory environment together with extensive industry research. *Solvency II: Stakeholder Communications and Change* is an essential text for all involved in Solvency II implementation. This revised edition has been updated to reflect developments in the Solvency II world and illustrate current challenges faced by affected entities.

The primary audiences for this book are the army of delivery partners who will make Solvency II a reality – programme directors, programme managers, project managers, actuaries, specialist support staff (press officers, communication managers, HR and market research experts), ERM managers, interim managers and consultants and – on the external front – EU insurance regulators, country regulators and industry lobby groups.

The secondary audiences for this book include international insurers and reinsurers who do business in the EU and who are subject to its regulatory system, and those in the global financial services industry who are not directly affected at the moment but who may face similar regulatory regime change in the future.

FOREWORDS

FOREWORD BY TREVOR MATTHEWS

Solvency II will introduce a common, European-wide approach to prudential regulation. This more market-consistent and risk-sensitive regime which has been in development for over a decade will radically affect the supervision and operation of insurers and reinsurers across the continent.

While capital requirements are a central theme, Solvency II is also much about organizational, operational and behavioural changes – it requires changes in *how we do things around here* to ensure that effective risk management, governance and reporting are embedded throughout the organization. Everyone in the firm needs to be making decisions based on the organization's risk appetite.

The full implementation of Solvency II requires a massive effort but the new system provides the framework for organizations to develop a new approach to decision making, to realize synergies and to create new products to meet the needs of changing markets.

As we enter the final countdown period, with the implementation date now set at 1 January 2016, Solvency II can be a trigger for introducing grassroots improvements. Adopting a holistic approach, which embraces organizational, operational and behavioural change will position your group to optimize the benefits from this historic development. Don't miss the opportunity!

Trevor Matthews,
Non-Executive Director at Bupa Australia,
Sydney

FOREWORD BY ADRIAN BALFOUR

Solvency II represents the greatest change for the European insurance industry in some 50 years. It will radically change the supervision of insurers and reinsurers across the whole of the European region.

Structured change management can help facilitate the organizational, cultural and people changes needed for successful Solvency II implementation so as to identify hidden risks, ensure adoption and maximize associated benefits. Good stakeholder management and communications ensure that disparate groups are engaged appropriately, with the right people getting the right messages at the right time, while activities that drive and embed culture transformation can increase adoption of Solvency II and enable benefits realization.

This book addresses a neglected niche in the market and explains how to address these important challenges. It tracks the progress of Solvency II, considering first how it originated and then explains how to manage organizational change activities to prepare for full implementation on 1 January 2016.

Embracing change is critical to survival and progress. To quote C.S. Lewis, 'It may be hard for an egg to turn into a bird; it would be a jolly sight harder for it to learn to fly while remaining an egg'.

Adrian Balfour,
Founder of PCubed and entrepreneur

ACKNOWLEDGEMENTS

To those many parties in the industry who have contributed to furthering understanding of what Solvency II implementation means for affected entities via forums and publications and whose input has helped shape my thoughts and this book.

To the host of independent contractors and delivery partners implementing the Solvency II framework, in particular Charis Adu Kwapong, Solvency II IMAP Lead and formerly of the FSA, and Andries Beukes, Solvency II Pillar 1 Lead and Director of Global Actuarial.

To my Publisher at Gower Publishing, Jonathan Norman, and his team for their drive and professionalism in bringing this book to the market.

TESTIMONIALS

Powerful, practical advice on how to take a strategic and people-focused approach to leading change so as to maximise benefits for the business. [O'Donovan] fills a neglected niche in the Solvency II literature, drawing on a variety of experiences, tools and techniques. While written in a Solvency II context, this book is relevant (and a must read) for anyone involved in managing change.

Andries Beukes,
Director, Global Actuarial

[O'Donovan] has succeeded admirably in writing an engaging and readable account, on what can be a difficult topic, whilst recognising and reinforcing the fundamental importance of Solvency II to the way in which insurers will do business in the future.

Robert Surridge, LL.B, MA, ACII,
Chartered Insurer, Solicitor,
co-author of *Houseman's Law of Life Assurance*
and contributor to *Insurance Disputes*

A very useful resource for any manager who needs to familiarise him or herself with Solvency II implementation.

Gary Chadwick,
former Solvency II Programme Manager, Friends Life

GLOSSARY OF TERMS

EU ENTITIES

AMICE	Association of Mutual Insurers and Insurance Cooperatives in Europe
CEA	Comité Européen des Assurances
CEIOPS	Committee of European Insurance and Occupational Pensions Supervisors
EC	European Commission
EIOPA	European Insurance and Occupational Pensions Authority
EIOPC	European Insurance and Pensions Committee
GCAE	Groupe Consultatif Actuarie/Européen
ICISA	International Credit Insurance and Surety Association

UK ENTITIES

ABI	Association of British Insurers
PRA	Prudential Regulatory Authority

OTHER TERMS

ARROW

Advanced Risk Responsive Operating frameWork: the risk-based Supervisory Review Process operated by the PRA in the UK. It is expected to be impacted by the introduction of Solvency II

BAU

Business As Usual

BRCC

Board Risk and Compliance Committee

CFO

Chief Financial Officer

COO

Chief Operating Officer

CRO

Chief Risk Officer

DA

Design Authority

IAIS

International Association of Insurance Supervisors: The IAIS issues global insurance principles, standards and guidance papers, provides training and support and organizes industry gatherings

ICAS

Individual Capital Adequacy Standards: this is the current capital adequacy requirements regime applicable to UK insurance firms. It will be replaced with the adoption of Solvency II on 1 January 2016

IFRS

International Financial Reporting Standards

IMAP

Internal Model Approval Process; mandatory for all firms seeking to use their own Internal Model

ISG

Insurance Standing Group: this is a regular pre-consultation forum for the FSA and Industry to discuss issues relating to Solvency II and any ad hoc domestic prudential policy issues

MCR

Minimum Capital Requirement: this is a key quantitative capital requirement defined in the Solvency II Directive

ORSA

Own Risk and Solvency Assessment: ORSA is the framework employed by a (re)insurance undertaking to identify, assess, monitor, manage and report the short and long term risks it faces or may face

PAQC   Pre-Application Qualifying Criteria; all firms entering the IMAP
                      process must go through PAQC first to qualify

Pillar 5   Regulators have adopted a Three Pillar Approach to Solvency II.
                      Adding Pillars 1 and 2 together has created what is commonly
                      referred to as Pillar 5

QIS   Quantitative Impact Studies: the QIS exercises test the financial
                      impact and suitability of proposed Solvency II requirements on
                      firms. There have been five, EIOPA run, full QIS exercises

RAG   Red, Amber, Green; status measurement system used by
                      programme and project management

RSR   Report to Supervisors: a report submitted solely to the
                      supervisor which contains the information considered necessary
                      for the purposes of supervision

SCR   Solvency Capital Requirement: the SCR is the higher of the two
                      capital levels required in Solvency II

SFCR   Solvency and Financial Condition Report: this is the public
                      disclosure report which is required to be published by all affected
                      entities. It will contain both quantitative and qualitative data

Standard   The general non-entity specific formula used by insurers to
Formula   calculate their Solvency Capital Requirement under Solvency II

CHAPTER 1

INTRODUCTION

The European insurance industry accounts for 33 per cent of the global market, making it the largest in the world. It is made up of a robust London market, the Continental Europe market, and the developing markets of Eastern Europe and Russia. Its business encompasses life insurance and general insurance, the former covering plans which relates to a person's life with the latter covering motor, health, property and all other types of non-life related risks.

The industry employs nearly 1 million people directly, and another million are outsourced employees and contractors. In 2012, it invested more than €7,400 billion in the global economy, life insurers paid out around €646 billion in benefits while non-life insurers paid out almost €313 billion. Total gross written premiums for the whole European market amounted to €1,100 billion. According to Insurance Europe, the European insurance and reinsurance federation, the sector has the largest pool of investment funds in the European Union, with almost €8,400 billion invested in the global economy in 2012. This is equal to 58 per cent of the GDP of the EU.[1]

Each European Union (EU) member state has its own insurance regulator. However, EU regulation sets a harmonized prudential regime throughout the whole of the Union. This is supervised by the European Commission (EC).[2]

1.1 EU SOLVENCY REGIME CHANGE

1.1.1 Background

The original EU solvency regime for the insurance industry was developed in the 1970s to provide a standard for monitoring the economic capital held.

---

1   European Insurance – Key Facts, Insurance Europe, August 2013. [Online]. Available at: www.insurancesurope.eu/ [Accessed: January 2014].
2   For more on the European Commission, turn to p. 27.

Solvency I defined the capital requirement by specifying simple, blanket solvency margins. Over time, inadequacies in the regime became apparent:

- It was not risk sensitive and could require entities to carry too much, or not enough, capital.
- Different application was allowed by different EU member states, allowing for significant divergence across territories, hampering cross-border regulation and causing regulatory arbitrage.
- Insurance solvency could not be judged based on information published.
- 'Good' behaviour was restricted.
- Financial conglomerates were not being regulated consistently.
- With accounting standards moving to a 'Fair Value' approach as part of the new International Financial Reporting Standards (IFRS), the need to improve consistency between published accounts and solvency valuations gained momentum.

These issues led to the development of Solvency II.

1.1.2 The Solvency II Regime

Solvency II is a fundamental review of the capital adequacy regime for the European insurance industry.[3] It's a major EU Directive and applies to all EU-based insurers and reinsurance entities with gross premium incomes exceeding €5 million or gross technical provisions in excess of €25 million.[4]

The aim of Solvency II is to establish a revised set of EU-wide capital requirements and risk management standards which will replace current requirements. The objectives of the European industry for Solvency II are as follows:

1. To align capital requirements with the underlying risks of an insurance company.
2. To maintain strong, effective policyholder protection while achieving capital allocation.
3. To develop a proportionate, risk-based approach to supervision with appropriate treatment both for small companies and large, cross-border groups.
4. To provide incentives to insurers to adopt more sophisticated risk monitoring and risk management tools – this would include developing full and partial internal capital models and increased use of risk mitigation and risk transfer tools.

---

3   Delivering Solvency II, Issue 1, Financial Services Authority, UK, June 2010. [Online]. Available at: www.fsa.gov.uk/ [Accessed: September 2010].
4   www.fsa.gov.uk/.

5. To achieve a harmonized approach to supervision across all EU markets – this will help to ensure there is a level playing field for all insurers and should provide a common standard of protection to all consumers regardless of the insurers' legal form, size or location.

6. To increase competition within EU insurance markets and the global competitiveness of EU insurers – reducing or removing unnecessary regulatory constraints and adopting a coherent 'lead supervisor' approach for pan-European groups. This will provide more choice and a better deal for EU consumers, and also enable EU insurers to compete more effectively in global insurance markets, in line with the Lisbon agenda.[5]

Solvency II sets out new, strengthened EU-wide requirements on capital adequacy and risk management for insurers. When it comes into effect on 1 January 2016, it is expected to reap the following benefits:

- more protection for policyholders;
- reduced risk of market disruption;
- better risk-based capital assessment through the use of Internal Models and a closer link between capital and risk;
- best practice risk management and governance;
- a more informed and assured basis for decision-making;
- industry homogeneity and alignment.

Solvency II has been created in accordance with the Lamfalussy process which is an approach used by the European Union for the development of financial service industry regulations. Originally developed in March 2001, it is named after Alexandre Lamfalussy, the chair of the EU advisory committee which created it. The process is composed of four 'levels', each focusing on a specific stage of the implementation of legislation:

- Level 1: framework principles: developing a European legislative instrument (or Directive) that sets out core values and essential framework principles, including implementing powers for detailed measures at Level 2.
- Level 2: implementing measures: sector-specific committees and regulators developing more detailed implementing measures (prepared by the EC following advice from the Committee of European Insurance and Occupational Pensions Supervisors (CEIOPS))[6] that are needed to operationalize the Level 1 framework legislation.

---

5   Solvency II – Understanding the Process, CEA, February 2007. [Online]. Available at: www.cea.eu/ [Accessed: September 2010].
6   On 1 January 2011, CEIOPS was replaced by the European Insurance and Occupational Pensions Authority (EIOPA).

- Level 3: guidance: CEIOPS working on joint interpretation recommendations, consistent guidelines and common standards. CEIOPS also conducting peer reviews and comparing regulatory practice to ensure consistent implementation and application.
- Level 4: enforcement: more vigorous compliance and enforcement action by the Commission is underpinned by enhanced cooperation between member states, regulators and the private sector.

Ironically, the Lamfalussy process was established to fast track regulation implementation but, given how many years it is taking to implement Solvency II, one cannot help but wonder what the slow track process would look like.

Although there is no reference to 'pillars' in the Directive, Solvency II has become synonymous with the 'Three Pillar Approach' adopted by CEIOPS to help frame the regulatory review process:

- Pillar 1 focuses on quantitative requirements such as valuing assets, liabilities and capital.
- Pillar 2 focuses on supervisory activities which provide qualitative review through the supervisory process including a focus upon the company's internal risk management processes.
- Pillar 3 addresses supervisory reporting and public disclosure of financial and other information by insurance companies.

To use an everyday analogy, Pillar 1 is about checking out a car by its appearance, Pillar 2 is about checking under the bonnet for a closer examination while Pillar 3 is about allowing the neighbour around to inspect it.

Solvency II		
Pillar 1	**Pillar 2**	**Pillar 3**
Quantitative Requirements	**Qualitative Requirements**	**Disclosure Requirement**
Solvency Capital Requirements (SCR) Minimum Capital Requirements (MCR)	Supervisory review of internal controls and risk management	Supervisory reporting and market disclosure

Figure 1.1   The three pillars of Solvency II
Source: PricewaterhouseCoopers.

Recently, data management has emerged as the 'hidden pillar'. With this approach, Solvency II sets out new Solvency Capital Requirements (SCR) and Minimum Capital Requirements (MCR). The SCR represents the normal target level of capital for an insurer while the MCR is the absolute minimum threshold whereby, should a company fall below this level, they will be forced to cease writing business.

The formulae used to calculate the SCR will include the risks outlined below, with correlations between each risk integrated into the calculations:

- Insurance and Reserve Risk – risk arising from insurance contracts. It relates to the uncertainty about the result of the insurer's underwriting.
- Catastrophe Risk – related to potential losses associated with major catastrophes that have been insured against.
- Interest Risk – exists for all assets and liabilities of which the net asset value is sensitive to changes in the term structure of interest rates or interest rate volatility.
- Equity Risk – arises from the level or volatility of market prices for equities and assets associated with these prices.
- Currency Risk – covers the volatility of currency exchange rates.
- Spread Risk – originating from financial instruments, explained by the volatility of credit spreads over the risk-free interest rate term structure.[7]

When calculating their capital requirement under Solvency II, organizations have a choice of which model to use – the *Standard Model*, the *Internal Model* or the *Partial Model*:

- The Standard Model is a default formula available to all companies.
- Internal Models are firm specific calculations designed to maximize capital efficiency. They must encompass all the risks present in the standard model, but can be built to capitalize on the entity's unique composition and inherent risk diversification. As Internal Models are produced by the entities themselves, they require the approval of the local industry regulatory before they can be used. This safeguard ensures that they capture all the risks within the standard model to an adequate degree.
- The Partial Model is an amalgamation of the Standard Model and the Internal Model. It will be attractive to smaller organizations who cannot meet the potentially prohibitive costs inherent in the construction of an entity specific Internal Model.

---

7   Solvency II Overview, Scandinavian Capital Solutions, 2010. [Online]. Available at: www.scandanaviancs.com/ [Accessed: February 2011].

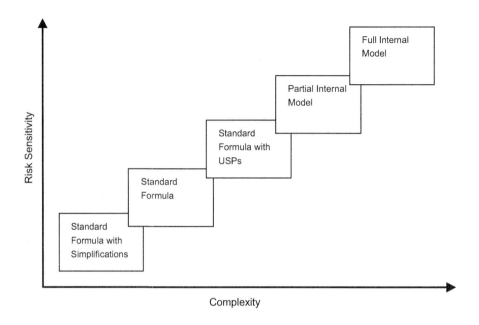

Figure 1.2   Progressive levels of sophistication in capital assessment
Source: Tim Edwards, 2010, Solvency II Challenges Facing the Insurance Market. [Online].
Available at: https://ktn/innovateuk.org [Accessed: February 2011].

A further option open to firms is to use the Standard Model, but provide its own calculations for certain risk modules. As with the Internal Model, this option requires local regulatory permission for its adoption by a given firm.

For those companies that have opted for a partial or full Internal Model, the 'use test' is a key requirement to consider as part of the Solvency II vision. At first glance, the requirements of the use test would appear to be quite straight: 'the Internal Model is widely used and plays and important part in their governance system'. But on closer inspection, it becomes clear that this stipulation will represent major cultural change as it spells out a requirement for executive management to use their model to make their decisions and to demonstrate this usage.

Another feature of Solvency II is the quantitative impact studies (or QIS) that have been carried out. Each QIS has served a particular purpose:

> *QIS1 was conducted in late 2005 to acquire insights into the potential impacts of the new solvency regime, with a particular focus on Pillar 1. QIS1 was concerned with the level of prudence in current technical provisions and allowed for feedback from insurers and reinsurers on the feasibility of initial standard model proposals. QIS2 built on the QIS1 results and focused*

on investigating the effect of the possible restatement of the value of both assets and liabilities under the Solvency II framework. It also investigated alternatives for setting the capital requirement (MCR and SCR). QIS3 built on the first two studies and was concerned with group and calibration issues and the implications of Solvency II on company-wide strategic structural decisions. QIS4 focused on the use of full and partial Internal Models. It also investigated further group related issues. QIS5 required firms to integrate the significant changes made to technical provisions in their submissions.[8]

1.1.3 The Impact of the Financial Crisis

As a result of the recent financial crisis, the economic environment entered its deepest post-World War II recession with all major economies and sectors affected; insurance fared better than banking.

The insurance industry operates on a very different business model to banks. For insurers and reinsurers, cash is in first with claims paid out at a later date whereas for banks, cash is paid out first with payback and interest collected at a later date. While the interbank market became undone, the main problem for the insurance industry was losses on investment portfolios and shareholder capital. The banking system veered close to a total collapse, requiring major government intervention, while the insurance industry continued on with business as usual, providing cover and honouring claims made. As a result, confidence in the banking sector has taken a heavy knock with serious reputational damage incurred, whereas trust in the insurance industry remains largely intact.

In a paper published by CEIOPS, some of the implications of the downturn were examined to gain insights on how Solvency II might best be implemented. Chief amongst its findings were the following:

- Solvency II should be adopted to allow for more transparent risk-orientated information on the soundness of EU insurers.
- Dependency structures underlying the standard formula may need to be strengthened.
- Governance, risk management and internal controls are potential weak points.
- Own risk assessment is crucial and may need reinforcing within the implementing measures.
- The scope of regulation for groups needed further thought.
- A point in time assessment of solvency will entail some level of cyclicity.[9]

---

8   Adapted from http:solvency-2.com/keypoints/qis.php [Accessed: January 2011].
9   Lessons Learnt from the Crisis: Solvency II and Beyond, CEIOPS, 27 March 2009.
[Online]. Available at: www.eiopa.eu/ [Accessed: December 2010].

These insights served to inform and shape the final EU Directive on Solvency II – Directive 2009/138/EC.

1.1.4 Countdown to 1 January 2016

The Level 1 Directive text was adopted by the European Parliament on 22 April 2009 and was endorsed by the Council of Ministers on 5 May 2009.[10] This concluded the legislative process and laid the groundwork for Level 2 implementation and Level 3 guidance. The full Solvency II regime is to be put into force on 1 January 2016 and Level 4 enforcement will be ongoing thereafter. Before then, a great deal needs to happen.

Further to the consultation on Level 2 which commenced in 2010, final advice was presented to the EC. The Commission was tasked with preparing the Level 2 implementing measures which were adopted in the autumn of 2011. Consultation on Level 3 guidance took place when Level 2 implementing measures were approved by the Parliament.

Official QIS 5 results were released by April 2011. According to CEIOPs, almost 70 per cent of all insurers and reinsurers submitted their results by the end of November 2010. This is a very high take-up rate. Across the European market, the Internal Model Approval Process is being rolled out by all local regulators in their home countries.

On 19 January 2011, the EC published its draft Omnibus II Directive which amended the Solvency II Framework Directive, to bring it in line with the EU's Lisbon Treaty. This new Directive had serious ramifications for the implementation timeline which had become something of a moveable feast. Firstly, and as expected, Omnibus II changed Solvency II's implementation date from 31 October 2012 to 1 January 2013 (it has since moved to 1 January 2016). Secondly, Omnibus II replaced Level 2 'implementing measures' with 'delegated acts' and 'implementing technical standards'. Thirdly, transitional provisions for key areas e.g. supervisory reporting and public disclosure are subject to different maximum deferral periods up to a maximum of 10 years.

The uncertainty brought about by Omnibus II placed the industry under a lot of additional pressure. According to an article on www.insuranceday.com dated 11 April 2011, industry confidence in implementation plans for the forthcoming Solvency II regime was recently dented 'with a series of warnings of potentially dire consequences arising from the existing implementation plans. Four industry groups, including the Comité Européen des Assurances (CEA), Europe's largest insurance association, wrote to the European Commission to voice concerns about developments in the Solvency II process.'

---

10   [Online]. Available at: www.fsa.gov.uk/ [Accessed: October 2010].

Things have moved on since and it would appear that we are at last on the homeward run. On 12 December 2013, the UK Prudential Regulatory Authority (PRA) published a supervisory statement to assist firms within the scope of Solvency II in their preparations for implementations. This statement came into effect on 1 January 2014 and ceases to operate on the day prior to implementation of Solvency II. The Quick Fix Directive published in the Official Journal of the European Union on 18 December 2013 came into force on 19 December 2013, extending the implementation date of the Solvency II Directive to 1 January 2016. The deadline for transposition into national law is extended to 31 March 2015. Member states will be empowered to give Solvency II regulatory approvals from 1 April 2015. The Commission aims to publish delegated acts this summer (2014). Implementing technical standards are expected to be produced in three waves, with the first wave due to be adopted in October 2014. Affected UK organizations must submit their annual ORSA supervisory report to the PRA from January 2014 onwards.

Table 1.1   Countdown to Solvency II

	2014	2015		2016
Governance	Demonstrated progress to NCA of compliance with effective governance and risk management requirements **From Jan 2014**	Increased expectation from NCA of compliance with effective governance and risk management requirements **From Jan 2015**		Full compliance with effective governance and risk management requirements **From Jan 2016**
ORSA	First annual ORSA report to NCA **During 2014**	Annual ORSA report to NCA **During 2015**		Annual ORSA report to NCA **During 2016**
Pillar 3		Submission of 2014 annual returns 20 (solo) / 26 (group) weeks after year end 2014	Submission of first quarterly returns 8 (solo) / 14 (group) weeks after Q3 2015	Quarterly returns 8 (solo) / 14 (group) weeks after quarter end 2015 annual returns 20 (solo) / 26 (group) weeks after YE 2015
Internal Model pre-application	Internal Model pre-application process 2014 to mid-2015	Internal Model Application and Approval Mid to late 2015		

Source: Adapted from January 2011, *Solvency II, Bulletin* Vol. 19, Association of British Insurers, UK. Available at: www.abi.co.uk [Accessed: January 2014].

1.1.5 Lessons Learnt from Basel II

Often called the Basel II of the insurance industry, Solvency II is also based on three pillars (as illustrated in Figure 1.1). However, while Basel II was based on the recommendations of banking supervisors and central bankers from 13 countries regarding international standards for measuring the adequacy of a bank's capital, with Solvency II the European Commission is working jointly with EU member states to establish a solvency regime which is better matched with the evolved insurance environment. So while the architectural similarities of Basel II and Solvency II cannot be refuted, they should not blind us to some fundamental differences between the two, as outlined in the table opposite.

There is a lot that the insurance industry can learn from the banking sector's implementation of Basel II. The insights below are taken from a Solvency II programme management perspective and while they may be taken retrospectively for some of the more well-established programmes, they do provide useful pause for reflection:

- Firstly, make the business case for change, articulating both the regulatory drivers and the commercial benefits sought at any early stage to ensure, critically, that the Solvency II change is viewed as a change programme. This will position the programme director to successfully gain executive buy-in to the change programme and obtaining senior executive sponsorship. The sponsor is likely to set up a steering committee which will be responsible for setting the strategic direction of the programme and overcoming obstacles to change.
- Establish programme management and governance. Understand the division of responsibilities for all activities, in particular gap analysis and design, plus the build and implementation of solutions across the group and ring-fence full-time resources for the project, hiring subject matter experts to help shape and advise the programme. Understand the critical path and inter-dependencies, prioritize work accordingly and implement strong documentation disciplines.
- It is never too early to engage the regulator; many banks engaged with the regulator early on Basel II. This helped them to influence the debate in the face of uncertain regulation and understand how the Directive would be applied and they have seen the benefits over time.
- Experience has shown that greater commitment and success is gained and greater value delivered to the business if the change programme seeks to deliver business benefit not simply compliance.[11]

---

11   Adapted from The Same but Different, Deloitte, 2007. [Online]. Available at: www.deloitte.com/ [Accessed: November 2010].

Table 1.2   Comparison of solvency regimes: Solvency II v. Basel II

	Solvency II	Basel II
Objective	Protect policyholders against bankruptcy	Reduce systemic risk in the banking industry
Method	Mostly principle-based	Mixture of principle-based and rule-based
Scope	Applies economic principles to both assets and liabilities	Concentrates primarily on assets
Main risk covered	Underwriting, counterparty default, market and ALM, operational	Credit, market (as per BI), operational
Approach	Standard formulae or Internal Model (full/partial)	Standard or internal approach (full/partial)
Risk Models	Integrated approach	Separate models for credit, market and operational risk
Diversification	Explicitly allowed	Mainly included in general calibration

Source: A. Tiwari, CEO, Aptivaa Consulting, 22 February 2008, Solvency II. [Online]. Available at: www.aptivaa.com [Accessed: November 2011].

1.2 CHAPTER SUMMARY

The European insurance and reinsurance industry is currently undergoing major regulatory change, courtesy of a recent EU Directive. The focus on the change is the industry solvency regime. The original regime, 'Solvency I', was created in the 1970s to provide the industry with a shared standard for monitoring the economic capital held. Inadequacies in the model led to the development of Solvency II which represents a fundamental review of the capital adequacy regime for the industry. It is a major EU Directive and all EU-based insurers with gross premium incomes exceeding €5 million or gross technical provisions in excess of €25 million must comply. Solvency II promises to create a more transparent and professional picture of an entity's solvency position, provide greater protection to policyholders and lead to a more secure insurance market.

Solvency II has been developed in line with the Lamfalussy process which is an approach used by the European Union to develop financial services regulations. The process is made up of four levels that focus on different stages of legislation implementation Also, while there is no reference to 'pillars' in the EU Directive, CEIOPS has based Solvency II on three pillars as an aid to help entities implement Solvency II. In addition, firms will have a choice of employing a Standard Model provided, developing their own Internal Model or employing a Partial Model approach. Firms need to weigh the pros and cons to decide on the best approach for their environment.

The architecture of Solvency II is based on that of Basel II, a banking regulatory regime change relating to international standards for measuring the adequacy of a bank's capital. Both models are based on three pillars, but there are fundamental differences. For example, while the objective of Solvency II is to protect policyholders against bankruptcy, the objective of Basel II was to reduce systemic risk in the banking industry. Also, with Solvency II risk models are considered using an integrated approach while with Basel II, separate models are used for credit, market and operational risk.

Lessons learnt from the recent financial crisis have been the focus of a study conducted by industry supervisory group CEIOPS. Their findings underscored the need for Solvency II and served to inform the design of the EU Directive.

The Level 1 Directive text was adopted by the European Parliament on 22 April 2009, laying the groundwork for Level 2 implementation and Level 3 guidance. The full Solvency II regime is to be put into force on 1 January 2016 and Level 4 enforcement will be ongoing thereafter.

CHAPTER 2

INDUSTRY IMPACT AND RESPONSE

Solvency II represents a sea-change for the insurance industry. It will have a major impact on individual entities and the EU insurance and reinsurance industry as a whole, with its reach spreading further to the global markets.

2.1 SOLVENCY II AND AFFECTED ENTITIES

The impact faced by insurers and reinsurers is multifaceted. In the longer term, business strategies can expect to feel the effects of the new solvency regime change. As of 1 January 2016, the impact will be on governance, organizational decision-making, reporting, document control and interaction with supervisors. In the immediate future, however, the impact is very much on everyday life as the organization aligns to the Directive.

2.1.1 The Business Impact

While the nature of the impact on the business may only become apparent long after January 2016, proactive work needs to be done upfront to try to identify what this might look like so that steps can be taken to seize on opportunities and mitigate risks. Key business impacts identified by international management consultants 'Oliver Wyman'[1] include financial strength and flexibility, investment strategies, pricing, product features and competitor profile:

- *Financial strength and flexibility* – with the implementation of Solvency II, the financial position of a given organization will change in the future. This development needs to be studied to divine knock-on effects on business issues such as risk appetite and required profitability levels. Groups will need to consider the consolidated position and the impact of Solvency II on major entities and internal capital flows. Larger organizations will be able

---

1   L. Ziewer and O. Wyman, adapted from 'Assess the Business Impact of Solvency II', 4 November 2009.

to deploy the resources to develop more sophisticated systems that suit their unique profile; this should help them better assess and manage their risks and lower capital charges.

- *Investment strategies* – some investment strategies will incur higher capital charges under Solvency II and may not compensate for this by higher returns. Life insurers, for example, have a duration mismatch – holding assets with shorter duration than their liabilities – this does not look attractive in a Solvency II world.
- *Pricing* – rates increases will be necessary to compensate for any additional capital requirements; for example, the pricing of many investment guarantees is expected to become more expensive.
- *Product features* – current standard product features may attract unwelcome capital charges and this may lead to a change in products offered.
- *Competitor profile* – as corporate structures impact the ability to use capital efficiently, competitors may change their structures to maximize benefits. Also, some markets will become more attractive and others less so leading to a shift in competitor focus. And finally, not all companies will be able to develop their own Internal Model and derive the benefits expected for such an approach.

Solvency II will have a significant impact on the strategy and performance of affected entities. The fifth impact study (QIS5) is a key means for insurers and reinsurers to identify how they will be affected by the new regime.

2.1.2 Impact on Business-as-Usual

The more immediate impact of Solvency II will be on how the business is organized. Affected entities will require a more formal approach to governance, organization and decision-making. They will need to be able to demonstrate that risk awareness has been embedded into the fabric of the business.

Governance
In the Solvency II world, Board and executive management must show a stronger understanding of their firms risk appetite and capital implications and demonstrate references to both as part of decision-making. This means that Boards will need to understand and endorse what could be new and unfamiliar quantitative and qualitative information as part of their responsibilities as 'fit and proper' managers of the business. To manage market perceptions, investor relations teams will also need to ensure that financial and regulatory disclosures are compatible and, where they are not, be able to explain why not.

Organization
Firms will be required to have risk management, internal control, internal audit and actuarial functions in place if they do not already. They will also need to

look at how to coordinate these functions and wider business functions more closely.

Decision-making
Data and analysis techniques used within the business will need to reflect that being used in group solvency calculations, and vice versa.

Reporting
Solvency II will remove the multiple basis currently in place for solvency reporting and there will be greater onus on firms for more frequent and robust risk and capital reporting. To meet the reporting timeframes, changes may be required to policies, processes and systems, and how teams are organized.

Documentation
Greater discipline will be required on documentation, controls and disclosure. Greater transparency of approach to key risks and material assumptions underpinning the approach will also be required.

Interactions with supervisors
Solvency II enhances the powers of supervisors; CEIOPS provided a good platform for the sharing of policy views, and firms will now liaise with the ongoing platform for supervision – EIOPA.

Resources
The Solvency II framework will also require more complex and extensive analysis, along with a more systematic approach to risk management. This has increased the demand for actuarial and risk management skills.

Individual companies will be affected by Solvency II in different ways, based on their product mix, their use of reinsurance and the quality of their risk management and capital requirement models.[2] But for the industry as a whole, Solvency II represents major organizational change that will reverberate from the front line to the Board of directors, and from business units to the back office. Such a substantial change management initiative needs to be commissioned, managed and controlled accordingly to maximize benefits and mitigate risks.

2.1.3 Impact during Implementation

As Solvency II is implemented it will impact business-as-usual (BAU); this impact may be minimal, or it may be significant. If change is not managed,

---

2   Outlook, Ernst and Young, January 2010. [Online]. Available at: www.ernstandyoung. com/ [Accessed: November 2010].

it could result in interpersonal conflict, turf wars, wasted resources and disruptions to product and service delivery. Getting the right result means planning and resourcing the implementation programme accordingly. Grouping all Solvency II projects under an umbrella programme helps to achieve synergies and promote alignment. A clear and transparent governance structure communicates to the business overall accountability. Clear role definition with due consideration for existing roles in the business defines boundaries and helps avoid any related conflict, while the management of culture, change and communications issues helps ensure we bring the people with us as we forge ahead. These are just some of the best practices that firms can take to limit the impact on BAU during implementation, and promote maximum synergies.

2.1.4 Solvency II: A Crisis or an Opportunity?

Across the EU, common themes thread the industry response to the Solvency II Directive, although the responses of individual entities on a given issue can sit at opposite ends of the spectrum. According to a PricewaterhouseCoopers survey,[3] for some the new regime presents a crisis while for others it presents an opportunity. Some see it as strictly a compliance programme while others hope to gain serious business benefits in the longer term. The majority are focused on meeting the next implementation challenge, while only a minority is focused on the end game and gaining competitive advantage. Each entity is responding to the regulatory requirement based on its own profile, vision and capability.

In the survey which was designed to capture industry response and state of readiness, 115 companies (62 per cent write life insurance; 70 per cent write non-life and 16 per cent write reinsurance) from 22 countries shared how they are responding to Solvency II. The survey findings are condensed below with reflections on the implications of the findings added to provoke thought on issues that may need to be addressed by individual entities.

Long-term v. short-term view
The survey found that while respondents were keen to capitalize on the opportunities presented by Solvency II, and go beyond basic compliance, most were focused internally on operations. This suggests a 'fire-fighting' or reactionary approach to this major regulatory change as opposed to a proactive and planned change management approach.

---

3   Getting Set for Solvency II, PricewaterhouseCoopers, November 2010. [Online]. Available at: www.pwc.com [Accessed: December 2010].

Stakeholder management
As most projects were largely internally focused they were not engaging with external stakeholders (other than regulators and lobby groups). Without active engagement it would be difficult to influence key parties.

Internal communications
More than 40 per cent had no defined internal communications strategy for their implementation programme. Again, without active engagement, it would be difficult to change behaviours and instil an appropriate risk culture. A lack of engagement, both internally and externally indicates a lack of regard for broader stakeholder interests.

Competitive advantage
Only 25 per cent of respondents saw Solvency II as a way to gain a competitive edge and these were generally larger organizations. Life insurers were more likely to see the benefits than non-life insurers or reinsurers. Given the resources that are being spent on implementing Solvency II, more needs to be done to envisage business benefits and capitalize on these.

Cost savings
Seventy-six per cent of respondents were looking for a strong convergence with Enterprise Risk Management (ERM) to save on costs and gain business and operational benefits.

Executive sponsorship
Fifty per cent of projects were driven by the Board of directors/Board committee or the CEO (that is, they are business driven). The remaining 50 per cent were driven by back office functional heads (for example, the CRO, CFO or COO). Of the 18 per cent who indicated two project sponsors, the most usual combination was the Board, together with the CEO or CRO. Where a dual sponsor situation existed, and where both sponsors were from back office functions, additional risks to be added to the programme risk register included a potentially weakened position in terms of driving change and overcoming resistance, plus the possibility of turf wars and empire building. To mitigate the former, secure visible and consistent CEO support for the accountable executive sponsor. To mitigate the latter, get the sign-off of the Board on the governance structure together with governing principles would ensure that the structure on paper was a transparent reflection of the structure as it is lived and breathed in everyday practice. Any changes to the governance structure should go through a formal change control process which includes a revisiting of the governing principles and that is signed off by the Solvency II Steering Group.

Project organization
The majority have adopted a centralized approach to Solvency II implementation. Also, nearly 60 per cent have organized their programmes around the three pillars rather than business line or risk type. Where there are multiple businesses, there will be a need to do a business-line read across.

Resources (human and financial)
The survey found that many were focusing on the challenge of securing the right skills as opposed to a focus on the end game. There was a concern over a lack of availability of skilled internal resources.

The biggest challenge
Most saw ORSA as the biggest challenge in implementing Solvency II with Internal Model approval being second overall. Across Europe, groups have gone through Internal Model pre-approval processes with their home supervisors (just over one third of respondents are seeking Internal Model approval).

Project status and confidence to be ready on time
None of the more advanced respondents were 'very confident' that they would be ready on time; in effect, the level of confidence appears to reduce as the project progresses indicating a heightened awareness of the challenges of implementing Solvency II.

In 2013, Moody Analytics conducted their own Solvency II Practitioner Survey with 45 insurers of all sizes across Europe – and based in the UK, Germany, France, Italy, Spain, Denmark, Finland, Norway, Switzerland, Czech Republic, Slovenia and Malta. Their findings make for an interesting read. At one end of the spectrum, large firms have embraced Solvency II as an opportunity to enhance their capabilities and infrastructure, while at the other end of the spectrum there are firms addressing the requirements as a superficial regulatory 'tick-box' exercise. Those who take the latter approach could fail to take advantage of this opportunity to embed an enhanced risk culture that is aligned with Solvency II.

In terms of progress towards Solvency II, some 24.5 per cent are 'ready' (processes and solutions already running but not yet compliant), 64.5 per cent are 'developing' (solutions identified but not yet in full production), 11 per cent are 'late' (in the early stages of developing Solvency II capabilities). None of those surveyed were found to be 'compliant' (standard formula, partial or full Internal Models have been reviewed and approved by the regulator).

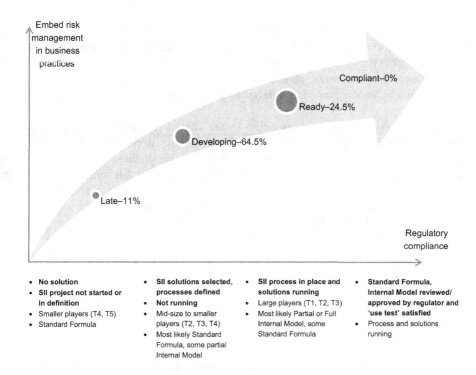

- **No solution**
- **SII project not started or in definition**
- Smaller players (T4, T5)
- Standard Formula

- **SII solutions selected, processes defined**
- **Not running**
- Mid-size to smaller players (T2, T3, T4)
- Most likely Standard Formula, some partial Internal Model

- **SII process in place and solutions running**
- Large players (T1, T2, T3)
- Most likely Partial or Full Internal Model, some Standard Formula

- **Standard Formula, Internal Model reviewed/ approved by regulator and 'use test' satisfied**
- Process and solutions running

Figure 2.1   Solvency II programme status: July 2013

Source: Adapted from Moody's Analytics, 2013, Solvency II Practitioners' Survey, Exhibit 9, p. 10. Available at: http://www.moodysanalytics.com/2013solvencyiisurvey [Accessed: January 2014].

Other findings and best practices observed include the following:

- Those insurers that have leveraged the regulation to define a data strategy have already started to yield benefits for their business, beyond regulatory compliance. These insurers have significantly improved (1) the quality and timeliness of decisions-making and (2) the understanding of the business and the risks affecting the firm.
- Those insurers at the more advanced stage of Solvency II implementation have embraced automation as a key catalyst to meet ongoing reporting requirements and concurrently running the business. However, many insurers are still using highly manual processes.
- To overcome the need to run internal actuarial models on a regular basis, some insurers are using high performance computing grids or applying proxy solutions such as Least Square Monte Carlo Modelling to optimize model performance while producing materially accurate results quickly and frequently.

- Those at the most advanced stages of implementation have an effective project sponsor who has influenced the change and driven the organization's progress towards compliance.
- Insurers at the more advanced stage of Solvency II implementation are using technology as a key catalyst to strengthen the firm's risk culture.

How individual entities are responding to the challenge posed by Solvency II implementation will determine the scale of benefits they derive in the long term. If they fail to plan strategically or resource their programme adequately, or if they treat Solvency II as strictly a compliance initiative, this will undermine the potential for adding value to the business and strengthening the competitive position. Solvency II will expect a substantial effort from affected entities – there is no way around this – but, if affected entities have the vision, resources and capability to meet the challenge, they can expect to maximize benefits.

2.2 SOLVENCY II AND THE EU MARKET

2.2.1 A Costly Burden or a Global Benchmark

Solvency II will change the ground-rules of European insurers by bringing risk awareness to the forefront of how businesses are judged by regulators, investors and customers.[4] It promises to increase the competitiveness of EC insurers and leave non-EC insurers behind.

However, concerns have been expressed that the scale and complexity of implementation and ongoing operation of Solvency II may put the EU market at a disadvantage in relation to non-EU competitors. Regulatory overload topped the list of risks facing insurers in a survey conducted by the Centre for Financial Services Innovation[5] with Solvency II being cited as a particular concern for some. One respondent, the head of group risk at a large life company, commented that 'the main risk is that Solvency II (despite great promise initially that would be a truly risk-based and economic framework) turns out to be a political compromise that ends up costing billions to implement and results in perverse incentives and unintended consequences for industry'.

More recently, European insurance groups such as the CEA are raising concerns that insurers who are already wrestling with the financial fallout from the global debt crisis, might not be in a position to meet Solvency II's requirements.

---

4   Countdown to Solvency II, PriceWaterhouse Coopers, January 2007. [Online]. Available at: www.pwc.com/.
5   Banana Skins survey, Centre for Financial Services Innovation in association with PricewaterhouseCoopers, May 2007. [Online]. Available at: www.pwc.com/.

In a report, 'Why Excessive Capital Requirements Harm Consumers, Insurers and the Economy,'[6] the CEA warned of the 'macro-economic effects of imposing excessively prudent capital requirements on the European insurance industry' under Solvency II. The CEA was concerned that industry regulators might default to excessively conservative standards, adding 'prudence on top of prudence', and that the implementing measures proposed by CEIOPS may result in a return to the out-dated and simplistic approach of Solvency I. The CEA's fears reinforce the findings of others that Solvency II's requirements may be too much, too soon.

Whether Solvency II becomes a costly burden or a global benchmark for best practice largely depends on the flexibility and responsiveness of its operation. The Association of British Insurers (ABI) has for one warned against 'arbitrary constraints that frustrate innovation and inhibit competition'.[7] The ABI was particularly keen to promote a single group supervisor and a 'principles-based regime that provides a secure framework for policyholder protection, while giving insurers the freedom to manage their own business as they see fit'. These elements are now enshrined in Framework Directive.

2.3 BEYOND THE EU

2.3.1 Equivalence to Solvency II

The notion of 'equivalence to Solvency II' is used in three distinct areas in the Solvency II regulations:

- Equivalence of reinsurance supervision (172);
- Consolidating non-EU subsidiaries into EU group Solvency II (227);
- Reliance on group supervision from outside the EU (260).

All three areas have the basic goal of ensuring that 'third-country equivalent regimes' provide a similar level of policyholder and beneficiary protection to the one provided under Solvency II. Note that countries and not companies are assessed for equivalence. A country assessed with respect to equivalence needs to 'go for' all three, and the verdict may indeed be different across the three for a single country.

---

6   Why Excessive Capital Requirements Harm Consumers, Insurers and the Economy, CEA, Brussels, 2010. [Online]. Available at: www.cea.eu/.
7   Media release following 'ICAS 2007 and the Path to Solvency II', March 2007. [Online]. Available at: www.abi.co.uk/.

The candidates for equivalence in the first wave were Bermuda, Switzerland and, for reinsurance, Japan. On 26 October 2011, EIOPA published final reports on their third country equivalence assessments, concluding that all three regimes mostly comply with Solvency II, with Bermuda's supervisory regime causing additional challenges. Most companies in Bermuda are said to have good Internal Models in place already, Switzerland is expected to be deemed Solvency II equivalent, while Japan is on its way to developing a regulatory regime similar to Solvency II. The United States is not expected to be deemed equivalent in the first wave, meaning European companies will need to apply Solvency II standards to their US businesses, and vice versa.

2.3.2 Assessing the Impact

Although Solvency II is a European Union initiative, it will have a far reaching effect beyond the EU.

Non-EU subsidiaries of EU groups
Under Solvency II, EU groups are required to calculate consolidated Solvency II results covering their global insurance business, including their overseas operations. Solvency II requires that either (i) the application of all Solvency II detailed calculations to that non-EU business or (ii) that the subsidiary be in a jurisdiction where the regulatory regime has been certified by the EU as being 'equivalent' to Solvency II. Where equivalence does not exist, the European parent will require considerable more information from the local subsidiary that will amount to additional reporting. But where the local regime has been judged equivalent, Solvency II will mean little extra work for the local subsidiary.

EU subsidiaries of non-EU groups
The EU operations of non-EU groups must submit and satisfy stand-alone ('solo') Solvency II requirements. Also, the group must submit a consolidated filing. This requirement may motivate the group to consolidate its EU operations into one legal entity where multiple entities exist.

Recognition of reinsurance from non-EU reinsurers
While Solvency I had an oversimplified treatment of reinsurance, affected entities will no longer face arbitrary limitations in the benefit resulting from their reinsurance. Under Solvency II, the impact of reinsurance and other risk mitigation techniques is now given full consideration. To be eligible for a reduction in capital requirements, reinsurance must be held with an EU-domiciled reinsurance company, one based in a regime deemed equivalent or one that is capitalized to a certain level.

2.4 CHAPTER SUMMARY

While the nature of the impact of Solvency II on the business may only become apparent long after 1 January 2016, work needs to be done upfront to try to identify what this might look like in order to seize on opportunities and mitigate risks. Key business impacts identified by consultants Oliver Wyman include financial strength and flexibility, investment strategies, pricing, product features and competitor profile.

For many affected entities, implementing Solvency II will represent major change and if this change is not managed, it could disrupt product and service delivery. Across the EU, common themes thread the industry response to the Solvency II Directive, although the responses of individual entities on a given issue can sit at opposite ends of the spectrum. For some, the new regime presents a crisis while for others it presents an opportunity. Some see it as strictly a compliance programme while others hope to gain serious business benefits in the longer term. According to research conducted recently by Moody's Analytics on progress towards Solvency II, some 24.5 per cent of firms have processes and solutions running but are not yet compliant, 64.5 per cent have identified solutions which are not yet in production, while 11 per cent are in the early stages of developing Solvency II capability. Each entity is responding to the regulatory requirement based on its own profile, vision and capability.

Solvency II will change the ground-rules of European insurers and promises to increase the competitiveness of EC insurers and leave non-EC insurers behind. However, some are concerned that the scale and complexity of implementation and ongoing operation of Solvency II may put the EU market at a disadvantage in relation to non-EU competitors.

Also, and although Solvency II is an EU initiative, it will have a far reaching effect beyond the EU. For example, under Solvency II, EU groups are required to calculate consolidated Solvency II results covering their global insurance business, including their overseas operations. EU operations of non-EU groups must submit and satisfy stand-alone ('solo') Solvency II requirements and the group must submit a consolidated filing. And, under Solvency II, the impact of reinsurance and other risk mitigation techniques is now given full consideration.

CHAPTER 3

FRAMING THE STAKEHOLDER CHALLENGE

Most Solvency II programmes assessed by industry studies found them to be internally focused with little engagement with external stakeholders. Also, 40 per cent of programmes did not have an internal communications strategy. These findings suggest that structured stakeholder management and communication are being neglected and this does not bode well for good programme management, and getting the right results.

While internal communication targets general staff and focuses on employee engagement, stakeholder management is a much broader piece embracing disparate internal and external constituents and focusing on stakeholder engagement and issues resolution. For a programme to move towards structured stakeholder management and communications, the stakeholder challenge must be first scoped. Understanding who the different players are in the Solvency II arena will inform *whom* the organization interacts with based on their own unique profile while good stakeholder management practices will determine *how*.

The Solvency II stakeholder challenge is framed by the context – a regulatory regime change imposed by the EU Parliament on the EU insurance industry. Within this context, regulators and affected entities each face their own particular challenge.

The EC is tasked with implementing this EU regulatory regime change on hundreds of stakeholder groups across the industry, with the support of local regulatory authorities. Their objective is to *secure stakeholder compliance and buy-in* for the new regime change; this involves stakeholder analysis and stakeholder relationship management to log and mitigate stakeholder issues and concerns and provide them with ample opportunity to influence the design and implementation processes via public hearings and other appropriate consultation channels. The diagram overleaf (Figure 3.1) names key stakeholders involved in the formative stages of the Solvency II process, and indicates how different parties feed into it. In Section 3.1, each of these stakeholder groups is introduced in turn with their unique roles defined.

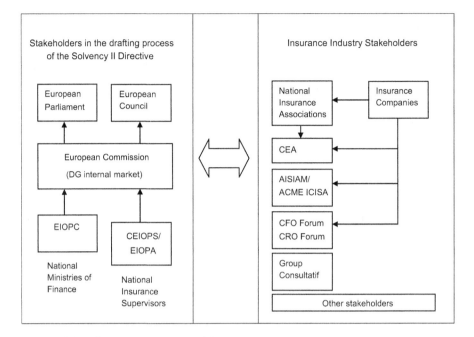

Figure 3.1   Solvency II stakeholders

Source: Adapted from 'Solvency II – Understanding the Process', CEA, February 2007.

For affected entities, their external-facing stakeholder management role exists for the purposes of gathering market intelligence on evolving Directive requirements and *demonstrating constructive involvement* in the design and implementation processes to industry regulators. This includes engaging with external forums for lobbying activity to shape the debate around final designs, implementation plans and other processes. The external facing stakeholder challenge also involves reinforcing market confidence in the organization's ability to implement Solvency II and secure compliant status. However, their internal-facing role is more similar to that of the Regulators because, internally, the entity is also imposing change on a broad range of constituents and seeking *to secure stakeholder compliance and buy-in*.

While Figure 3.1 provides clear insights into the stakeholder management challenge faced by Regulators, further investigation is required to develop a more complete and up-to-date picture on the stakeholder challenge faced by affected entities, not least because insurers and reinsurers face the Solvency II stakeholder challenge on two fronts – external and internal.

3.1 THE EXTERNAL STAKEHOLDER CHALLENGE

3.1.1 Regulators

European Parliament
The European Parliament (EP) is the directly elected parliamentary institution of the EU. It jointly passes legislation (such as Solvency II legislation) with the Council of Ministers. While its origins can be traced back to the 1950s, members of the Parliament have been voted in by their own peoples since 1979.

European Commission (EC)
The European Commission is the executive body of the European Union. It reports directly in to the European Parliament/Council and, in general, is responsible for proposing legislation, implementing decisions, upholding treaties and running the Union on a day-to-day basis. The EC is responsible for implementing Solvency II across the EU.

European Council
The European Council is the institution of the European Union (EU) responsible for defining the general political direction and the priorities of the EU. It is made up of the heads of state or heads of government of its member states and the Council President. While it has no formal legislative powers, the European Council deals with major issues and any decisions made are 'a major impetus in defining the general political guidelines of the European Union' (in general, the EC proposes new legislation, but it is the Council and Parliament that pass the laws).[1]

European Insurance and Pensions Committee (EIOPC)
EPIOC is made up of experts from the national Ministries of Finance. This body studies Solvency II implementing measures to create the legal text that will frame the operation of the new regime.

Committee of European Insurance and Occupational Pensions Supervisors (CEIOPS)
The role of CEIOPS (2003–2010) was to advise the European Commission on insurance regulation matters such as Solvency II implementing measures, helping implementation and facilitating cooperation between supervisors. CEIOPS was replaced by EIOPA on 1 January 2011 (see overleaf).

Local financial regulators
Local financial regulators supervise Solvency II implementation in their own jurisdiction. In the UK, the Financial Services Authority has now become two separate regulatory authorities – the Financial Conduct Authority (www.fca.org.uk) and the Prudential Regulatory Authority (www.bankofengland.co.uk).

---

1   www.wikipedia.com/European-Council/.

As a result, Solvency II-related responsibilities have passed to the Prudential Regulatory Authority (PRA). The PRA was set up by the Financial Services Act 2012 and is part of the Bank of England. It is responsible for the prudential regulation of banks, building societies, credit unions, major investment firms and insurers.

European Insurance and Occupational Pensions Authority (EIOPA)
Compared with its predecessor (CEIOPS), EIOPA has more powers to enforce prudential standards through the development of Binding Technical Standards (BTS) which are qualitative, or principles-based, rather than specific calibrations. EIOPA will have a more active part to play in the coordination of group supervision activities.

3.1.2 Lobby Groups

Comité Européen des Assurances (CEA)
The CEA represents the European insurance and reinsurance industry through national insurance associations in each of the European Union member states and eight other countries also. It coordinates Solvency II lobbying activities and represents members' views on issues under consultation. For a complete list of the CEA national association membership list, go to Appendix 1.

The Association of Mutual Insurers and Insurance Cooperatives in Europe (AMICE)
This body has been created in 2007 by merging the two Europe-based mutual and cooperative insurance associations – AISAM (which had around 120 direct members in 21 countries) had a global remit and ACME (which had 57 members in 19 countries) had a Europe-specific remit. AMICE works to ensure that its members' interests are taken into account in securing a level playing field for all insurers in Europe.

The International Credit Insurance and Surety Association (ICISA)
Founded in 1928 as the first ever credit insurance association, current members account for 95 per cent of the world's credit insurance business. They play a key role in facilitating trade and economic development on all five continents. The ICISA Solvency II Expert Group provides a forum for participants to maintain an awareness of regulatory developments and to exchange ideas on relevant issues.

The CRO Forum
The CRO Forum was formed in 2004 to work on key relevant risk management issues within the insurance industry. Members are large multinational insurance companies represented by their Chief Risk Officers who are considered industry leaders with respect to valuation, risk measurement, and risk management. The forum has three core aims which include the alignment of regulatory requirements with best practice risk management, the acknowledgement of group

synergies, especially diversification benefits, and the simplification of regulatory interaction.

The CFO Forum
The CFO Forum was created in 2002 and represents 20 large European industry groups. The aim of the forum is to influence, on behalf of its members, the development of financial reporting, value-based reporting, and related regulatory developments for insurance enterprises (such as Solvency II). The forum is attended by the Chief Financial Officers of major European listed (and some non-listed) insurance companies.

Groupe Consultatif (GCAE)
The Groupe was established in 1978 to bring together the actuarial associations in the European Union to represent the profession in discussions with the European Union institutions on existing and proposed EU legislation. Each of the 33 EU member states is represented in the Groupe.

Local industry associations
Insurance and reinsurance associations in the various member states for example, the UK's Association of British Insurers (ABI) and their Solvency II-focused working groups and committees.

3.1.3 The Markets

Investors
Investors may be individual shareholders or institutional investors. They regularly purchase equity or debt securities for financial gain in exchange for funding an expanding company. Examples of major institutional investors include Scottish Widows Investment Partnership Ltd, Schroder Investment Mgt (Institutional Group), MassMutual Financial (Investment Group), Pictet and Cie and State Street Global Investors (Institutional Group).

Analysts
A market analyst collects and analyses data to evaluate existing and potential product and service markets. It is their responsibility to identify and monitor competitors and research market conditions or changes in the industry that may affect sales. Credit analysts are concerned with bonds, while equity analysts are concerned with share price.

Ratings agencies
A credit rating agency assigns ratings to issuers of certain types of debt obligations as well as the debt instruments themselves. It takes into consideration the issuer's credit worthiness and affects the interest rate applied to the particular security being issued. It also affects the image and reputation of the entity issuing the

security. The value of such ratings has been widely questioned after the 2007/2009 financial crisis.[2] Once Solvency II goes live on 1 January 2016, the role of ratings agencies is expected to diminish as the powers of the EU supervisors are enhanced.

3.1.4 Special Interest Groups

Policyholders
These stakeholders hold policies with a given insurer or reinsurer. A policy with an insurance company will cover life and non-life, while a policy with a reinsurance company is held with the insurance company and is underwritten by the reinsurer. A key objective of Solvency II, from the Regulator's perspective, is increased policyholder protection.

The media
The insurance industry media encompasses trade publications, websites, online forums and all other channels used to promote industry news to turn a profit. It also embraces 'commentators' who are independent financial advisors (IFAs) and 'intermediaries' from the financial sector of the national media. The media's stake is a given firm's Solvency II programme will be in terms of how newsworthy developments are; the onus is on the firm to ensure that those developments that reach the light of day are positive ones.

3.2 THE INTERNAL STAKEHOLDER CHALLENGE

On the internal front, the stakeholder map for affected entities can be divided into four clusters of constituent groups – 'Programme Governance', 'Programme Committees', 'Directly Impacted Teams' and 'Indirectly Impacted Teams'.

3.2.1 Programme Governance

The Board
The Board is made up of executive and non-executive directors. The EU Directive makes the Board ultimately responsible for ensuring Solvency II compliance. To that end, local regulatory bodies are expected to examine individual Board members on topics such as their organization's risk appetite, how that impacts different parts of the workforce, and how the risk appetite has influenced strategic decision-making.

Parent Body Board
Where an insurance or reinsurance entity is part of a larger concern, a Parent Body Board will exist. The Parent Body's concern will be the impact of Solvency II

---

2   Adapted from www.en.wikipedia.org/wiki/Credit rating agency/.

on strategies, so if acquisitions are a key strategy then securing Solvency II compliance in line with peers will be of critical importance. In this instance, the Parent Body Board is likely to take a more hands on approach to deepen their understanding of Solvency II and progress made against plans.

Executive sponsor
Where the Solvency II programme is positioned as a business driven initiative, it will be sponsored by a business leader and will be financed by the operational plan. Generally speaking, this is the ideal situation as business leaders are usually better positioned to manage change and overcome resistance. It may be that the CEO is the sponsor with one of his/her direct reports (a business leader) chairing the Steering Committee. Alternatively, and where the Solvency II programme is positioned as a back-office driven initiative, it will be sponsored by one or more senior executives such as the Director of Risk and Compliance and/or the Director of Finance. Where multiple sponsors exist, one must act as the 'Accountable Executive Sponsor', that is, s/he is accountable to the Regulator for Solvency II progress against plans and final outcomes. While there are exceptions to the rule, driving change and overcoming resistance can be more difficult from this position as those acting as obstacles to change may be business leaders. In this scenario, strong public backing by the CEO for the 'Accountable Executive Sponsor' can help align the executive management team for the common cause.

Solvency II Steering Group
The Steering Group is responsible to the Board for ensuring the successful execution of Solvency II. Delivering on this will involve providing strong governance and direction to programme management, ensuring deliverables are to plan, resolving key strategic issues and overcoming resistance. Regulatory authorities may be looking for evidence that the Steering Committee makes decisions and at an appropriate level and that they do not exist simply as a 'rubber stamp' forum. In the UK, the Financial Services Authority (FSA) has already shown an interest in reviewing such evidence.

3.2.2 Programme Committees

The Board Risk and Compliance Committee (BRCC)
This is a Board delegated authority whose remit is to assist the Board in providing leadership, direction and oversight of the Group's management of risk and compliance. The BRCC will typically review any Solvency II programme materials destined for the Board/s, and will be the first point of call for sign-off, prior to Board approval.

The Design Authority (DA)
The remit of the Design Authority is to interpret Directive requirements and ensure the programme is structured to meet those requirements. The DA should be made

up of appropriate representation from impacted stakeholder groups to protect the integrity of the end-to-end solution. They should have control over any changes to Solvency II design at a Group level. To enable absolute clarity on the implications of any changes to Solvency II design, and the management of any such changes, have in place clear programme documentation to support the DA.

The Audit Committee
The Audit Committee typically reviews financial reports, financial decisions and oversees the implementation of new accounting principles or regulations. As the audit committee regularly interacts with the leadership team, it is in a position to comment on the capabilities of managers such as the CFO. Where accounting practices are brought into question, the audit committee make secure independent consulting resources to conduct an investigation where deemed necessary. External auditors are also typically required to report to the audit committee on a range of issues, such as accounting adjustments arising from their audits and any identified fraud or illegal activity. Solvency II requires that firms demonstrate the independent and authority of the Audit Committee.

3.2.3 Directly Impacted Teams

Staff who are directly impacted by the new solvency regime will be those who use capital in their day-to-day business and who will have to live with Solvency II requirements after it has been embedded.

Risk, compliance, audit and actuarial
Risk, compliance, audit and actuarial teams and functions may well be impacted by the new requirements related to how the business is structured and governed. Also, many organizations have taken the approach of nominating BAU team leaders from these areas to head up Solvency II programme workstreams so that they will own the new way of doing things in the Solvency II world.

Pricing
Where product portfolios are impacted by the new regime, so too will pricing policies. While it may be still too early to say what these impacts will look like, colleagues from pricing need to be kept very much in the loop so that they can understand strategic implications for the business.

IT
If the experiences of Basel II implementation are any indication, IT will be significantly impacted by Solvency II. While the nature of such impacts is discussed in Chapter 5, suffice to say at this point that the choice of the Standard Model versus Internal Model will play a significant part in IT requirements and how the regime change impacts IT staff.

Delivery partners
Delivery partners include permanent staff, consultants, professional interim managers and contractors. On large programmes, all are likely to be employed, working in partnership with each other to deliver on the common goals. Delivery partners will be directly impacted in the immediate future as their roles will be shaped by the Solvency II requirement.

3.2.4 Indirectly Impacted Teams

Indirectly impacted staff do not use capital in their day-to-day business and will not be at the receiving end of directly-related internal restructuring, resulting from Solvency II.

General staff
That said no one is completely immune from Solvency II. For example, creating a Solvency II risk culture is not something which can be done in isolation with a pocket of staff such as Finance and Risk communities. And sales staff will be impacted at some point by changes to policies and products. Therefore, the broader workforce should receive Solvency II communications on the Solvency II regime, its benefits, key dates, the organization's risk appetite and how that impacts the organization.

3.3 CHAPTER SUMMARY

For the European Commission which is imposing this regulatory change on behalf of the European Parliament, the stakeholder challenge is enormous and involves liaising with a broad range of EU industry groups in order to secure compliance and commitment. For affected entities, the challenge is perhaps more complex as they face the stakeholder management challenge on two fronts. The first involves working with external stakeholders groups, at both EU and national level, to demonstrate capability to deliver on Solvency II and secure compliance status. The second front is the internal one; as securing Solvency II compliance will involve imposing significant internal change on affected entities, a broad range of internal stakeholders will be impacted and will need to be managed. These include the Board/s, Solvency II Committee/s and Steering Groups, directly impacted teams and indirectly impacted ones.

CHAPTER 4

THE SOLVENCY II 'CULTURE TEST'

Solvency II is not just about capital. It is a change in behaviour.
Thomas Steffen, Chairman of (CEIOPS)[1]

It has been said that too many companies are approaching Solvency II as a bottom-up technical analysis against the technical requirements instead of taking a strategic approach, identifying what needs to change, how change will be delivered and how it will impact the workforce. However, since early 2011, the tides have been turning. Managing organizational change is firmly on the Solvency II agenda.

4.1 UNDERSTANDING CULTURE

A key impact of Solvency II on people is the embedding of a risk culture which measures up to the Solvency II requirement. Successful delivery will depend on a sound understanding of culture, on what makes a risk culture, on what the Solvency II requirement is and how to pass the Solvency II 'culture test'. The benefits of successful delivery include:

- Board convincing Regulator that a Solvency II risk-culture is embedded across the organization;
- Ongoing business decision-making reflecting a risk-conscious approach, making for a sounder business.

4.1.1 Defining Culture

So, what *is* culture? According to Marvin Bower, former Managing Director of McKinsey consulting practice, culture is '*how we do things around here*' (1966).[2]

---

1   European Commission media release, 10 July 2007.
2   Marvin Bower, *The Will to Manage*, McGraw-Hill, 1966.

Bower's popular one-liner is very useful for general discussion on the topic as it captures some key aspects of culture that persons from all backgrounds can understand (that is, shared behaviours typical of a specific community). But to successfully embed a particular type of culture or to tackle culture transformation, a more detailed definition is necessary so that one can get to grips with the different facets of culture enabling one as to identify any gaps in a given culture and apply appropriate interventions. For such purposes, culture can be defined as:

> *An organic group phenomenon, whereby tradition passes on acquired learning to successive generations, while innovation builds capacity to evolve with the environment. The interplay between these complimentary forces manifests in the shared beliefs and assumptions of the workforce. It is visible in attitudes, behaviours and artefacts, and determines the quality of business outcomes and results.*[3]

Culture is created by a given community as it problem-solves and strives to meet the needs of the group in the face of environmental challenges. In the organizational context, this problem-solving process will be shaped by organizational needs also and will result in specific products, services and experiences that meet market demand. As part of the culture developmental process, shared learning experiences lead to the creation of a shared paradigm of beliefs and assumptions that determine 'how we do things around here'.

Table 4.1   The levels of culture

Drivers	Needs ▼	*Community Needs* – What we require as a group to be happy, productive workers; needs generate emotions, motives and energy which can be positive or negative.	*Organizational Needs* – What the organization needs to survive and thrive (these needs should drive group problem-solving and learning).
	Central Paradigm ▼	The network of shared beliefs (principles and values) and assumptions from which people derive meaning and understanding of their world.	
Expressions	Attitudes ▼	Pattern of shared attitudes in relations to people, places and things.	
	Behaviours ▼	Pattern of shared behaviours in relation to people, places and things, including daily routines and the means deemed acceptable for achieving the ends.	
Reflections	Artefacts ▼	Artefacts include symbols of the past and present, and those which represent what the company aspires to.	
	Results	Outcomes and results are a function of the prevailing culture and either reinforce or explode the beliefs and assumptions stakeholders hold on the espoused culture.	

Source: Adapted from G. O'Donovan, *The Corporate Culture Handbook*, 2006.

---

3   G. O'Donovan, *The Corporate Culture Handbook*, The Liffey Press, Ireland, 2006, p. 45.

Most of the time, such beliefs and assumptions are unconscious – we are not even aware of them – but, make no mistake, they influence attitudes and behaviours which in turn drive particular outputs, outcomes and results. When aligned with organizational needs, shared beliefs and assumptions lead to desired outcomes and results. But when such alignment does not exist, there is a gap between the everyday practice (or the prevailing culture), and the required (or espoused) culture. Where this is the case, outcomes and results will miss the mark. The drivers, expressions and reflections of culture have a cause and effect relationship that is captured in the model opposite.

Edgar Schein (senior lecturer at MIT Sloan School of Management) identified a range of *embedding mechanisms* that serve to *reinforce* culture:

- What leaders pay attention to, measure and control;
- How leaders react to critical incidents and organizational crisis;
- Observed criteria by which leaders allocate scarce resources;
- Deliberate role-modelling, teaching and coaching;
- Observed criteria by which leaders allocate rewards and status;
- Observed criteria by which leaders select, promote, recruit and excommunicate organizational members;
- Organization design and structure, systems and procedures;
- Organizational rites and rituals;
- Design of physical spaces, facades and buildings;
- Stories, legends and myths about people and events;
- Formal statements of organizational philosophy, values and creed.[4]

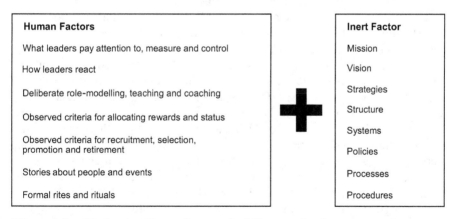

Figure 4.1   Understanding culture embedding mechanisms

---

4   Adapted from E. Schein, *Organisational Culture and Leadership*, 2nd Edition, Jossey-Bass, USA, 1992, p. 231.

On reflection, these mechanisms can be divided into two categories as illustrated in Figure 4.1 on the previous page. Human factors relate largely to leadership behaviour while inert factors are non-human organizational mechanisms, with 'policies' incorporating creeds, charters, philosophies and 'processes' incorporating rites and rituals.

While in the 1970s and early 1980s it was believed that embedding mechanisms (and inert ones particularly) drove culture, it is now widely understood that culture drives embedding mechanisms with the Board and executive management team setting the tone at the top; for if a community does not buy into any particular policy or process, and so on, the culture will quite simply reject it and work around it. Whichever point of view one subscribes to, the important thing to remember is that both culture and embedding mechanisms should be aligned. Finally, culture embedding mechanisms serve to reinforce the culture. But they are not the culture. So before one can even think about which levers might be appropriate for embedding a risk culture, one must first consider the very essence of a risk culture, a point lost on some major consultancies as they flog their wares in the Solvency II world.

4.1.2 Risk Culture Defined

So, what is a risk culture and how does it relate to other types of culture which one hears about in the corporate context for example, a 'service culture', a 'culture of ethics', a 'culture of innovation' or a 'health and safety culture'?

Let's consider the concept of the 'risk culture' first. We established earlier that culture is driven by particular beliefs and assumptions that shape attitudes and behaviours at all levels of the organization. What beliefs and assumptions drive a 'risk culture'? This is a fundamental and critical question because our answer will determine if, for example, we are talking about a 'risk adverse culture', a 'risk management culture', a 'risk aware culture' a 'risk conscious culture' or a 'risk aggressive culture', for each is underpinned by different operating assumptions. As risk is integral to the insurance industry, clearly a 'risk adverse culture' will not support the business. The term 'risk management culture' doesn't say a lot, as there are good and bad management practices, while a 'risk aware culture' does not capture the need to be risk conscious when making decisions. And a 'risk aggressive culture' is what laid the foundation for the recent credit crisis. Therefore, a sense of prudence, coupled with an appreciation of the organizational need to survive and thrive in an evolving environment, would suggest that embedding a 'risk conscious culture' is the appropriate target. In a risk conscious culture, managers thoughtfully decide, based on risk parameters set.

Secondly, when we talk about a 'service culture', 'a culture of ethics' or any other type of culture, we are in fact focusing on just one facet of a given culture, but that facet has been deemed critical to the survival of the organization at a particular point in time. This gives it primary importance over other facets of the culture. In fact, a 'culture of ethics' and a 'risk culture' can (and should) coexist. Which facet reigns supreme at any particular time should reflect the environmental challenges the organization faces and where it needs to place most resources and energies to survive and thrive. This is exactly what is happening in the financial services industry at the moment where embedding a 'risk culture' has gained priority over other cultural challenges such as creating a service culture. But do bear in mind that the risk culture will sit within the broader organizational culture e.g. the Aviva culture or the Legal & General culture so, where possible, ensure that work on the risk culture is developed in line with work on the organizational culture and values.

Figure 4.2   The risk culture framework

A risk culture is based on particular beliefs and assumptions. These can be clustered according to specific cultural tenets, namely risk, integrity, governance and leadership, decision-making, empowerment, teamwork, responsibility and adaptability, as illustrated in Figure 4.2 overleaf. These tenets are expressed in everyday workplace practices via attitudes and behaviours and, when they are expressed by leaders, they serve as powerful (human) culture embedding mechanisms. The upper segments of Figure 4.2 show those tenets that make up the culture itself, while the lower segments show those inert mechanisms that will help embed the culture. Note that a Solvency II risk culture can be *reinforced* via great many policies, processes and procedures, and so on, that are detailed in the Directive. But make no mistake – these mechanisms are not the risk culture itself and will be embedded only if the culture is aligned and supportive.

4.1.3 The Directive Requirement

Now that we have a common language for discussing culture, we can turn our attention to the Directive and supporting material to consider the regulatory requirement and how it can be satisfied.

While the word 'culture' in not to be found in the Directive, the word has emerged in the draft supporting material entitled 'Level 2 Implementing Measures' which was published in 2010. Also, the Directive itself hints at the subject of culture. Take Article 44, for example:

> *Insurance and reinsurance undertakings shall have in place and effective risk-management system comprising strategies, processes and reporting procedures necessary to identify, measure, monitor, manage and report, on a continuous basis the risks, at an individual and at an aggregated level, to which they are or could be exposed, and their interdependencies. That risk management system shall be effective and well-integrated into the organisation structure and in the decision-making process of the insurance or reinsurance undertaking with proper consideration of the persons who effectively run the undertaking or have another key function.*[5]

Article 44 talks about 'strategies, processes and procedures' and the need to 'identify, monitor, measure, manage and report risks'. In the language of culture, 'strategies, processes and procedures' are *culture embedding mechanisms*. The other items should be interpreted as *shared behaviours* because it is ultimately people that will make judgements, manage risks and make decisions – and not inert systems. This point becomes clear in the Level 2 draft text (Article 251 SG3)[6] which state the need for '*appropriate reporting procedures and processes*

---

5   EU Directive, 2009/138/EU/Article 44.
6   EU Article 251 2SG, Commission Level 2 Draft Regulation, 2011.

to ensure that information on the material risks faced by the undertaking and the effectiveness of the risk management system is actively monitored and analysed and that appropriate modifications to the system are made'. Clearly, while inert systems will play a central role, it is people who will monitor, analyse and modify the system – and yet the industry focus is on the 'use test' which, while important, is more narrow in the greater scheme of things.

Notice that there is no reference to the shared beliefs, assumptions and attitudes that constitute the required culture and enable the culture embedding mechanisms. By applying the concepts behind the 'levels of culture' model in Figure 4.1 to Article 44 we can see in Figure 4.3 that what the Directive refers to is but the tip of the iceberg, with the engine that is the risk culture submerged beyond our view. Only by tackling the levels of culture submerged below the waterline and below our line of sight will the embedding mechanisms have any real effect.

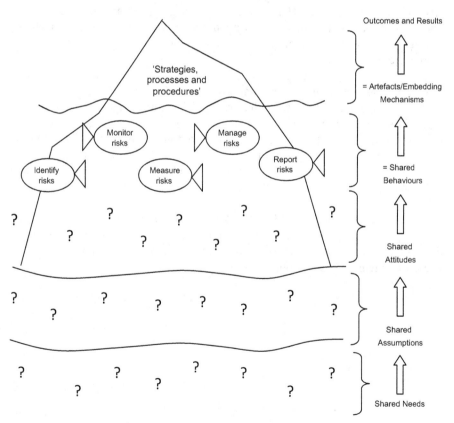

Figure 4.3   The Solvency II Directive and culture

Turning next to the Level 2 Draft Regulation, we can find the first direct reference to culture in Article 257 SG5[7] which relates to the internal control system. This article has a requirement for '*an appropriate culture and environment that supports internal control activities*'. This is a reference to the 'leadership and governance' aspect of the culture which must be driven by the Board who set the tone. In fact, throughout the Directive and supporting material there are a great many references to embedding mechanisms that will *support* a risk culture. But, at this juncture, little is being said in the evolving support material about the make-up of the risk culture itself.

4.2 EMBEDDING A RISK CONSCIOUS CULTURE

While, for Solvency II, the 'use test' has been a central industry focus (demonstrating how model outputs are used to inform decision-making around areas such as business planning, capital management and capital allocation, and risk monitoring and oversight), it is the 'culture test' that will determine whether or not Solvency II is embedded in a given organization and if the above-mentioned happens. For it is people who will adopt the inert systems, manage risks and make decisions, based on their particular set of beliefs and assumptions.

Those beliefs and assumptions supportive of a Solvency II risk culture are illustrated in Figure 4.4 using the 'cultural inventory approach' to culture analysis so as to provide a helicopter view. Using this approach, alternative beliefs and assumptions are presented on a continuum in relation to a specific cultural tenet, with those supportive of a risk (conscious) culture highlighted with a star for easy reference. This inventory can be used to stimulate discussion and debate.

By exploring these beliefs and assumptions an organization can develop a risk culture philosophy, a set of guiding principles which reflect appropriate beliefs and assumptions, and which will inform its risk management activities; an example statement is shared in Figure 4.5.

---

7   EU Article 257 SG5, Commission Level 2 Draft Regulation, 2011.

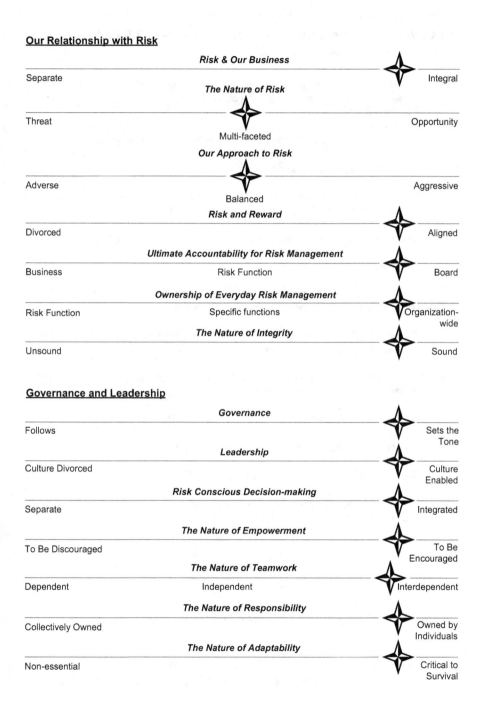

Figure 4.4   Characteristics of a risk culture

SOLVENCY II RISK CULTURE PHILOSOPHY STATEMENT

- Any risk can represent a threat, an opportunity or an unknown. In our organization, all risks are communicated and appreciated for what they are with appropriate action taken.

- When considering risks, we thoughtfully decide based on risk parameters set.

- We are incentivized to do the right thing.

- The management of risk is ultimately owned by the Board and, as such, cannot be fully delegated to the CRO or elsewhere for that matter.

- Across the organization, conscious risk management is accepted as part of everyone's role and responsibility and we each have a part to play in the three lines of defence risk management system.

- Integrity is the essential fabric of all that is moral, sound and whole and is a core principle upon which our beliefs and assumptions rest.

- We meet the Solvency II requirement for an appropriate 'tone at the top' with our management providing appropriate organizational values and priorities.

- We nurture an organizational culture that enables and supports the effective operation of a system of governance.

- We take various risks into account when making capital based decisions in particular.

- We are empowered, enthusiastic, responsible and productive.

- We are respectful of our service chain and internal customers.

- We take personal responsibility for our actions, in particular the risks we take and decisions we make.

Signed by Chief Risk Officer _____

Figure 4.5   Solvency II risk culture philosophy statement

Herein, each of the beliefs and assumptions that underpin a risk culture are discussed in detail, with example embedding mechanisms suggested for each.

4.2.1 Our Relationship with Risk

Risk and our business
Risk is integral to insurance and reinsurance business – without risk there is no
business. In a risk conscious culture, risk is an accepted part of the business, but
it is balanced within defined parameters that constitute the organizations 'risk
appetite'. This risk appetite is communicated to all within the context of business
strategies and goals so that all are aligned and staff understand how risk exposures
should be assessed for likelihood and impact. Also, the risk function is involved in
strategic planning activities, investment and divestment decision-making and the
design of organizational goals and performance measures. When risk is divorced
from business planning activities, this leads to bad decisions and heightens the risk
profile of the organization.

Table 4.2   Risk and our business

Supportive culture embedding mechanisms	
Inert factors	**Human factors**
• Establishment of risk function; • Appointment of CRO with appropriate authority; • Effective information and communication procedures; • Adequate monitoring systems; • Risk culture philosophy; • Risk management framework; • Communications.	• Leaders at all levels are seen to manage risk as part of managing the business; • Leaders communicating risk appetite within the context of business strategies and goals; • Risk function involved in strategic planning activities, investment and divestment decision-making and the design of organizational goals and performance measures.

The nature of risk
Any risk can represent a threat, an opportunity or an unknown. While risk has come
to be seen as a threat by many in the current operating environment, appreciating
the multi-faceted nature of risk enables people to have a healthy relationship with
it. Creating such an environment requires leaders to set the right tone at the top
by embracing, alongside good news, reports of risks that may represent bad news
or the unknown. The danger of leaders discouraging the latter is that it can lead to
staff being ignored, punished and even fired for raising such reports. This, in turn,
is sure to lead to poor risk mitigation and expose the organization to losses. In the
risk conscious organization, all risks are communicated and appreciated for what
they are with appropriate action taken.

Table 4.3   The nature of risk

Supportive culture embedding mechanisms	
Inert factors	**Human factors**
• Mechanism which allows staff to anonymously report risks (this will demonstrate appreciation for all risks and overcome any current adversity to reporting risks that are not good news); • Informal processes on responding to risk reports aligned with the formal processes; • Risk culture philosophy; • Risk management framework; • Communications.	• Leaders graciously accepting reports of risks that may represent a threat or the unknown; • Staff encouraged to report all kinds of risks; • Reports of threats and hazards to strategy embraced and responded to appropriately; • Leaders seen to raise reports on risks that represent bad new or the unknown, and to manage them appropriately; • Story-telling by leaders on the multi-faceted nature of risk.

Our approach to risk
When considering risks, managers thoughtfully decide based on risk parameters set. In a healthy risk culture, the community is not risk adverse but risk conscious. While the risk adverse culture will be heavy on controls and compliance, the risk conscious culture fosters an environment whereby employees take a balanced approach and can confidently choose how to deal with a particular risk. A risk aggressive culture, on the other hand, will encourage employees to grab at risky deals that fall outside the organizations risk appetite without giving them due thought and consideration.

Table 4.4   Ou approach to risk

Supportive culture embedding mechanisms	
Inert factors	**Human factors**
• Risk management training that encourages critical thinking and decision-making; • Processes that allow for risks to move within defined parameters, rather than expecting them to remain static; • Risk culture philosophy; • Risk management framework; • Communications.	• Leaders at all levels apply critical thinking to risks presented, and make decisions within the organization's risk appetite and conscious of inherent risks; • Leaders coach and role-model on the above.

Risk and reward
Employees are incentivized to do the right thing. The Directive supporting material on risk and reward[8] is based on principles that seek to reward the right behaviour and avoid providing incentives for inappropriate activities. To embed this, leadership behaviour and formal incentive programmes should encourage long-term prudent conduct and punish unethical behaviour and repeated unsound decision-making, as rewarding inappropriate conduct sets a bad example for how employees should behave and sends the message that the company does not value risk management. This could well discourage employees from reporting incidences that need to be reported. Rewards for all employees from the Board to staff at grassroots should depend on whether or not their behaviour complies with the organization's strategy and risk appetite. Furthermore, executive management should be evaluated on their ability to promote appropriate risk-based decisions and indeed they will as part of the Solvency II compliance approval process. In addition to setting appropriate standards, organizations can create formal working channels and procedures for reporting incidents, and ensure that confidentiality is upheld. A lack of alignment between risk and reward mechanisms will be frowned on deeply by Regulators.

Table 4.5   Risk and reward

Supportive culture embedding mechanisms	
Inert factors	**Human factors**
• Performance management and reward mechanisms incentivize the right behaviour and punish reckless and unethical behaviour; • Whistle-blowing mechanism; • Code of Conduct; • Code of Ethics; • Risk culture philosophy; • Risk management framework; • Communications.	• Leaders informal approach to reward and punishment aligned with organizational policy and Directive requirements; • Leaders publicly reward and punish more notable incidents of appropriate and inappropriate risk-taking; • Leaders communicate relationship between effective risk management and how the individual's performance is measured.

Ultimate accountability for risk management
The management of risk is ultimately owned by the Board and, as such, cannot be fully delegated to the CRO or elsewhere for that matter. This fact is enshrined in Article 40[9] of the Directive which states that '*member states shall ensure that the administration, management or supervisory body of the insurance or*

---

8   EU Article 265 SG13, Commission Level 2 Draft Regulation, 2011.
9   EU Directive 2009/138/EC/Article 40.

reinsurance undertaking has the ultimate responsibility for the compliance, by the undertaking concerned, with the laws, regulations and administrative provisions adopted pursuant to this Directive'. Further to Article 120 of the Directive, there is a requirement that *'persons who effectively run the undertaking shall be able to demonstrate an overall understanding of the Internal Model and a detailed understanding of the parts for which they are accountable.'*[10] In terms of the risk management function, the Board must ensure that policies are clear, embedded and accessible and when setting strategy and formulating business plans, risk must be a key consideration for the Board. Regarding the role of risk, Article 259 SG7 of the Level 2 Draft Regulation states that this includes *'assisting the administrative, management or supervisory body and other management in the effective operation of the risk management system'*.[11]

Table 4.6   Ultimate accountability for risk management

Supportive culture embedding mechanisms	
Inert factors	**Human factors**
• Structure, policies and practices reflect that the Board is ultimately accountable for risk management; • Risk function positioned as expert advisor to CEO and Board; • Risk champions identified and positioned across the organization in business partner role; • Risk culture philosophy; • Risk management framework; • Communications.	• The Board championing risk management in line with the Solvency II Directive; • CRO acting as expert advisor to the CEO and the Board.

Ownership of everyday risk management
Across the organization, conscious risk management is accepted as part of everyone's role and responsibility. All employees understand that risk and compliance rules apply to everyone as they pursue their goals, and they clearly understand, as appropriate, the risk appetite of the business. The 'three lines of defence' system embeds this ownership while ensuring risks taken on are in line with agreed policies. The three lines of defence are the Business (1st line), the Risk and Compliance functions (2nd line) and Internal Audit (3rd line). The first line is made up of staff across the business who are responsible for risk in their everyday roles. The second line is those departments who provide the tools and standards to enable the business to manage risks, and who provide guidance on how to

---

10   EU Article 213 TSIM3, Level 2, Commission Draft Regulation, 2011.
11   EU Article 259 SG7, Commission Level 2 Draft Regulation, 2011.

manage risks. The third line, Audit, provides independent assurance to executive management and the Board on the overall risk management framework. Too often it is the case that the risk function is fighting an uphill battle with the workforce believing that ownership for risk management lies with the risk function. The role of the risk function is to effectively collaborate with business units, coordinate data and advise business leaders.

Table 4.7   Ownership of everyday risk management

Supportive culture embedding mechanisms	
Inert factors	**Human factors**
• Code of Conduct reinforces that risk and compliance rules apply to everyone; • Training and educational programmes that reinforce desired culture; • Three Lines of Defence; • Mentoring programmes; • Policies and procedures; • Risk culture philosophy; • Risk management framework; • Communications.	• Leaders communicate via risk culture philosophy those beliefs and assumptions that underpin the organization's unique risk culture; • Leaders communicate the message that risk and compliance rules apply to everyone as they pursue their individual goals and objectives.

4.2.2 The Nature of Integrity

Integrity is the essential fabric of all that is moral, sound and whole. Article 42 of the Directive lays down its 'Fit and Proper Requirements' while Article 263 SG11 of the Level 2 Draft Regulation,[12] which relates to the 'Fitness of a Person', has a requirement for integrity of character. According to the latter, the fitness of a person *'shall be assessed having regard to that person's professional qualifications, knowledge and experience. The person shall demonstrate that the person has exercised due skill, care, diligence, integrity and compliance with relevant stands of the area or sector in which the person worked in.'* People of integrity are honest and morally upright individuals. When they are leaders, their ethical stance of issues serves as the basic fabric upon which their organization's 'culture of ethics' is built. The less morally inclined are likely to pick and choose when to take an ethical approach while amoral individuals, on the other hand, have a complete disbelief in any sort of morality or ethical code. They lack empathy or remorse and are said to have an anti-social personality disorder. As such, they will not be able to appreciate the fundamental nature of integrity.

---

12   EU Article 263 SG11, Commission Level 2 Draft Regulation, 2011.

Table 4.8   The nature of integrity – a moral perspective

Supportive culture embedding mechanisms	
Inert factors	**Human factors**
• A Code of Ethics that reflects everyday practices; • A whistle-blower mechanism that is utilized and respected by the workforce, with consequences for those who behave unethically; • Recruitment, selection and promotion processes; • Risk culture philosophy; • Risk management framework; • Communications.	• Leaders behaving in an honest and moral way; • Leaders reacting appropriately to examples of moral (or otherwise) conduct, particularly within their own ranks, demonstrating zero tolerance for unethical behaviour; • Leaders coaching staff on ethical practices.

Table 4.9   The nature of integrity – whole systems and processes

Supportive culture embedding mechanisms	
Inert factors	**Human factors**
• Aligned strategies and culture; • Risk culture philosophy; • Risk management framework; • Communications.	• A holistic approach that considers both the sum and the parts.

Table 4.10   The nature of integrity – a sound structure

Supportive culture embedding mechanisms	
Inert factors	**Human factors**
• Clear policy on governance that supports sound organizational structure; • Risk culture philosophy; • Risk management framework; • Communications.	• Leaders reacting appropriately to examples of standards and regulations being met (or breached), particularly within their own ranks.

4.2.3 Governance and Leadership

Governance
'*It is important that undertakings ensure an organizational culture that enables and supports the effective operation of a system of governance.*' With this one

statement, the Directive is underlining that culture is the driver for governance. Governance is culture-enabled – for better or for worse – a point driven home in 'A Board Culture of Corporate Governance'.[13] For when the culture is healthy and aligned with organizational needs it facilitates effective governance. When it is disconnected from business realities this can translate to, for example, a lack of alignment with environmental pressures such as regulatory and social change. A toxic culture can lead to corporate governance scandals, brand damage and a loss of investor confidence. The Directive draft supporting material[14] details the general governance requirements and those aspects that make up the system of governance.

Table 4.11   Governance

Supportive culture embedding mechanisms	
Inert factors	**Human factors**
• Formal risk management training and guidance; • System of governance; • Code of Ethics; • Risk culture philosophy; • Risk management framework; • Communication.	• Leaders communicate via risk culture philosophy those beliefs that underpin the organization's unique risk culture; • Leaders reacting appropriately to examples of good or poor governance, particularly within their own ranks.

Leadership
Solvency II has a requirement for 'an appropriate "tone at the top" with the administrative or management body and senior management providing appropriate organizational values and priorities'. Leadership paves the way for the workforce by role-modelling those attitudes and behaviours that are supportive of strategies and goals. The leadership team must articulate the culture and values for the workforce and role-model appropriate behaviours if good management practices are to be taken seriously through the ranks. Such behaviours include championing key initiatives, fulfilling formal obligations, respecting agreed policies and processes and acting in accordance with the risk culture philosophy in particular. When any member of the leadership team fails on any of the above, they set a bad example for the workforce that undermines the whole governance process.

---

13   G. O'Donovan, Change Management: A Board Culture of Corporate Governance, *Corporate Governance International*, vol. 6, no. 3, September 2003.
14   EU Article 257 SG5, Commission Level 2 Draft Regulation, 2011.

Table 4.12   Leadership

Supportive culture embedding mechanisms	
Inert factors	Human factors
• Training for leaders to all levels of the organization on leadership skills; • Succession planning based on system of governance; • System of governance; • Risk culture philosophy; • Risk culture framework; • Communications.	• Deliberate role-modelling, teaching and coaching on organizational culture and values; • Leaders paying attention and control to how the strategy is implemented, measuring progress along the way; • Leaders reacting appropriately to examples of good or poor leadership, particularly within their own ranks.

4.2.4 Decision-making

People take various risks into account when making capital-based decisions in particular. While most organizations would say that they take risks into account when making decisions, the reality is that this is often not the case or, where it is the case, it is based on the varying risk management skills of individuals. Organizations with a risk conscious culture encourage a discussion and review of risk scenarios that can help management and the Board understand risk issues. Such a process can develop the knowledge, skills and confidence of executives, enabling them to be more assertive and make better decisions. To strengthen the decision-making process, conduct a review of decision-making authorities as, sometimes, it can happen that middle managers have decision-making authority beyond their role that could present a major risk to the organization. Or it can happen that staff are fearful of being 'shot down in flames' for making a decision (see 'The Nature of Empowerment') creating a culture of indecision.

Table 4.13   Risk-conscious decision-making

Supportive culture embedding mechanisms	
Inert factors	Human factors
• Complete and appropriate risk data shared in a timely manner; • Discussions held as a matter of form on risk issues in relations to decisions on the table; • Review of decision-making authority; • Risk culture philosophy; • Risk management framework; • Communications.	• Board members understand type of risks faced by the business, the scale of risk and the risk appetite; • CRO and other executives available to discuss risk issues; • Leaders role-modelling, teaching and coaching.

4.2.5 The Nature of Empowerment

Empowerment will inject enthusiasm, encourage ownership and lead to better results. Empowerment is not just a word, it is a concept that must be brought to life through leadership example and supported through appropriate organizational policies and processes. Such tools enable people to use their initiative and to make decisions within clearly set parameters which protect both the individual and the organization from any grave errors. The Directive draft supporting material[15] is clear in its requirement for key functions to have the authority, resources, expertise and information necessary to carry out responsibilities. Where management are slow to empower staff and quick to criticize their contributions, the belief might prevail within the ranks that 'the less we do, the less mistakes we make and therefore the less trouble we can get into'. In such an environment, staff will be resistant to new responsibilities. They will keep their heads down to avert getting into trouble, they may turn up for work late and leave early if they can get away with it, morale will be low as will trust in the executive management team. This is a sure recipe for poor governance.

Table 4.14   Empowerment

Supportive culture embedding mechanisms	
Inert factors	**Human factors**
• Organizational design and structure – how power is shared and decisions made, for example, collectively or unilaterally by an authority figure; • Organizational systems and procedures that promote empowerment; • Clear roles and responsibilities; • Risk culture philosophy; • Risk management framework; • Communications.	• Leaders should react appropriately to examples of empowerment (or undermining) of colleagues, particularly within of their own ranks; • Deliberate role-modelling, teaching and coaching.

4.2.6 The Nature of Teamwork

A high-performance team is respectful of the service chain. Each team member understands that they do not work in isolation but form a vital part of a network where members rely on each other to get things done. This translates to cooperating, sharing information, building relationships and meeting formal obligations. Conversely when staff work in silos, withhold information and/or let

---

15   EU Article 258 SG6, Commission Level 2 Draft Regulation, 2011.

their colleagues down, this amounts to service failure and each incident chips away at the integrity of the service chain. This, in turn, has a very direct and negative impact on teamwork, relationships, productivity and results.

Table 4.15   Teamwork

Supportive culture embedding mechanisms	
Inert factors	**Human factors**
• Risk, Compliance, Audit and Actuarial teams working closer together; • Organizational systems and processes – for example, training on service chain mapping and the nature of interdependent teamwork; • Risk culture philosophy; • Risk management framework; • Communications.	• Appropriate criteria observed for allocating rewards and status, that is, management reward the team and/ or the individual, but not the individual only as this would undermine teamwork; • Regular social events held to facilitate good team relationships; • Formal team-building events held that are inclusive of interim managers, consultants and other external delivery partners; • Leaders reacting appropriately to examples of good or poor teamwork, particularly within their own ranks.

4.2.7 The Nature of Responsibility

In a risk-conscious culture, all employees take personal responsibility for their actions, in particular the risks they take and decisions they make. In the reverse scenario, when everyone is responsible, no one is responsible. This old adage drives home to us the specific nature of responsibility:

> *Once there were four managers*
> *– Everybody, Somebody, Anybody and Nobody.*
> *They were all busy people so when there was an important job to be done*
> *Everybody was asked to do it,*
> *But Everybody assumed that Somebody would do it.*
> *Anybody could have done it but Nobody did.*
> *When Nobody did it, Somebody got angry because it was Everybody's job.*
> *Everybody had thought that Somebody would do it,*
> *But Nobody realized that Nobody would actually do it.*
> *In the end, Everybody blamed Somebody when Nobody did what Anybody*
> *could have done.*
>
> (author unknown)

For responsibility to be real and tangible is must be specifically apportioned. Those made responsible for someone or something need to be aware of the fact and clear on how far their responsibility does or does not extend. If responsibility is shared on some level, this must be articulated to ensure that 'the buck stops somewhere'.

Table 4.16   Responsibility

Supportive culture embedding mechanisms	
Inert factors	**Human factors**
• Organizational design and structure – responsibility is specifically apportioned; • Organizational systems and procedures that promote taking responsibility; • Three Lines of Defence system; • Risk management framework; • Risk culture philosophy; • Communications.	• Leaders reacting appropriately to examples of staff taking (or shirking) responsibility particularly within their own ranks.

It would be remiss to discuss responsibility and accountability without a reference to the third part of the equation – authority. Generally speaking, employers are quick to assign responsibility and accountability too as organizations moved from being activity-centred to results-orientated in the face of a rapidly increasing rate of change in the environment. However, they can be sometimes slower to assign authority. Any post-holder needs a certain level of authority so that they have a platform for delivering on their responsibilities and making things happen. This is something to bear in mind when recruiting for Solvency II posts. A lot needs to be delivered, and people need to be given the authority to get on with the job within, of course, the parameters of clearly defined roles and responsibilities.

4.2.8 The Nature of Adaptability

Culture has a dual nature. It is constant, yet it is also inventive. Tradition preserves the group's distinct identity and way of life while ongoing innovation invigorates the culture and optimizes problem-solving abilities in the face of change (adapted from *The Corporate Culture Handbook*, G. O'Donovan, 2006). It is commonly understood that dinosaurs didn't survive because they didn't adapt to their changing environment. Adaptability is the key to survival. This means adapting to environmental forces of change by applying new innovations and new ways of doing things to solve new problems. We saw in Chapter 2 that organizations are responding to Solvency II differently. Some were strategic from the outset, keen to understand how the business might change because of Solvency II. Others have been more tactical, responding to the technical requirements and getting bogged down in the detail (unavoidable of course for actuaries involved in stress testing and QIS5 in particular). These varying responses are because of differing management capabilities and differing levels of ability to adapt to the new solvency regime based on the internal learning culture. In some organizations continuous learning at all levels of the organization is part of the fabric of how things are done, while in other organizations there is little appetite for learning. When the workforce is not abreast with external developments and new practices, its knowledge set becomes increasingly obsolete. Adaptability and an eye to the future is clearly an expectation of the Solvency II regime with Article 7 (2)[16] of the Directive laying out its requirement of organizations regarding *'future management action'* and *'expected future developments in the external environment such as demographic, legal, medical, technological, social, environmental and economic'*. Continuous learning and application of that learning is the fundamental enabler of adaptability.

Table 4.17   Adaptability

Supportive culture embedding mechanisms	
Inert factors	**Human factors**
• Strategies and plans based on clear view of external environment forces for change and Directive requirements; • Strategies and plans flexible to respond to environmental changes; • Change management training for all staff; • Policies and processes that embed continuous learning at all levels of the organization; • Risk culture philosophy; • Risk management framework; • Communications.	• Leaders paying attention to, measuring and controlling organizational learning activity; • Rewards and recognition for staff who further their education; • Team leaders sharing cross-functionally best practices and lessons on risk management in the Solvency II context.

4.3 STRATEGY AND TACTICS

Establishing and embedding a risk culture that is aligned with Solvency II is a strategic decision, and employing the tried-and-tested approach adopted for HSBC Hong Kong for the roll-out of an award-winning culture transformation programme[17] is probably a very good place to start. This approach is captured in Table 4.18. The activities mentioned therein will not necessarily run in sequence, and some activities are likely to run in parallel.

---

16   EU Directive 2009/138/EC/Article 77 (2).
17   'Together, We Win!' aka 'Chung Chi Sing Sing', winner of ASTD (USA) Award, 2005.

Table 4.18   Culture change: from vision to reality

1. Strategic Planning and Design	Back to the drawing board. Form the strategic management team. Create programme vision and define strategy. Organize the workforce. Design core programme and embedding mechanisms.
2. Strategy Implementation	Communicate programme vision and roll-out. Manage the human landscape. Maintain the momentum and solidify ground made.
3. Evaluation and Readjustment	Measure results and plan for the future.

Source: G. O'Donovan, *The Corporate Culture Handbook*, Figure 1, p. xxiv.

In the first instance, the organization needs to go back to the drawing board to consider the existing SII programme strategy and consider how the risk culture issue has been thought out, if indeed it has. Ensure that the revised strategy incorporates the risk culture component in a way which goes beyond culture embedding mechanisms/levers. Reallocate programme resources where necessary to reflect this new focus and, as goals and objectives are re-set, establish a baseline for the prevailing risk culture which will serve as a basis for measurement.

The strategic management team is likely to have already been established in the form of the Solvency II Steering Committee and the CRO is likely to be a member of this governing body. It is for this group to instigate a SII risk culture initiative, whatever shape or form that may take. Using the 'risk culture framework' presented earlier together with the supporting material, one can design the core programme and embedding mechanisms. During the implementation phase, the main challenge will be managing the human landscape and navigating the emotional dynamics of the workforce as people let go of the old and embrace the new e.g. those who have traditionally left risk management to the risk function will be experience culture shock. Another big challenge will be generating and maintaining momentum and solidifying ground made by rewarding those who make risk-based decisions in line with the established risk philosophy and culture. Communicate any such stories across the organization to show people what a risk culture looks like in practice and to establish role models who people can relate to. Measure the impact and effect of ongoing culture related activities with a view to determining how the gap is closing in terms of delivering on the Solvency II 'culture test'. The ultimate win will be of course securing Solvency II compliance status.

Embedding a risk culture that measures up to Solvency II is not going to happen overnight. So a useful approach to generating energy for the process is to establish some quick wins:

- First and foremost, get key stakeholders such as the Board, the CRO and programme Steering Committee behind you by establishing a dialogue that underscores the important of a risk culture. Also, respect the fact that a risk culture has already been established; the challenge will be to align with Solvency II requirements in terms of:
  - Culture (beliefs and assumptions that underscore particular cultural tenets);
  - Embedding mechanisms (aligning risk structure, policies, processes and so on in line with Solvency II requirements).
- Define the organization's risk culture philosophy and related messages. The risk culture philosophy is a statement which captures the organization's core beliefs and assumptions about risk (see Figure 4.5 for an example). To that end, conduct a series of workshops. In parallel to these sessions, engage the company Values team (either Strategy or HR) to ensure that the final risk culture philosophy and organization philosophy and values are aligned to face the future. Be sure too to link in to any upcoming company values roll-out or company brand roll-out programme.
- Use a range of internal communication vehicles to promote the risk culture philosophy and approved messages on the risk culture, highlighting that risk management is the responsibility of all and part of everyday responsibilities.
- Translate the risk culture philosophy into personal objectives and align incentives accordingly.
- Incorporate risk culture into Internal Model documentation and risk management framework before sign-off.
- Establish risk management educational and training programmes for Board members and leaders at all levels so that all are (i) aligned on the organization's approach to risk management, (ii) are clear on the organization's risk appetite, and (iii) understand the importance of walking their talk. Also, organize training to help staff understand model outputs and how to apply such output to decision-making.
- Establish a Code of Ethics that communicates company values (including risk related values), company expectations on ethics and standards and procedures.
- Establish a Code of Conduct that clarifies on company procedures for risk management (and other) management disciplines.
- Position risk champions to help business teams understand the risk culture and what kind of risk and capital information would help their decision-making in the Solvency II world.
- Conduct team-building sessions for business and risk teams to reinforce the culture and how they can best cooperation to implement the three lines of defence system.
- As individuals and teams behave in line with the risk culture requirements, reward and recognize such behaviour. Securing quick wins can generate interest and momentum amongst the ranks as the wider risk culture strategy is developed and roll-out.

Culture management is not unlike gardening in that it requires regular attention; the identification and pruning of unhelpful ways of doing things and the recognition and nurturing of more constructive ways. When it is left to its own devices, culture tends to end up like a garden overrun and strangled with weeds. When it is over-tended, the good can be chopped out with the bad. But when a balanced approach is taken to nurturing and pruning activities, that garden that is the culture can bloom and thrive.

4.4 CHAPTER SUMMARY

Embedding a risk culture will depend on a sound understanding of what culture is, on what makes a risk culture, on what the Solvency II requirement is on culture and how to pass the Solvency II 'culture test'.

Culture manifests in the shared beliefs and assumptions of the workforce; it is visible in attitudes and behaviours and it determines the quality of outcomes and results. Culture is embedded via leadership behaviour and also policies, processes and other organizational mechanisms but these mechanisms are not to be confused with the culture itself. Quite simply, if the community rejects any of the above-mentioned, it will not become part of the culture.

Article 44 of the EU Directive has a requirement for the establishment of a system necessary to identify, measure, manage and report, on a continuous basis, the risks, at an individual and aggregated level, to which they are or could be exposed and their interdependencies. It is people who manage risks and make decisions so the requirement is for a risk culture.

A risk culture is based on a particular set of shared beliefs and assumptions that rest on specific cultural tenets and promote a 'risk conscious' approach. These tenets are risk, responsibility, accountability, decision-making, leadership and governance, integrity, teamwork and empowerment. They are embedded in the risk culture framework (Figure 4.2) which can help organizations establish a risk culture by embedding appropriate beliefs, assumptions that will shape attitudes and behaviours, and choose appropriate interventions that will embed the risk culture.

CHAPTER 5

CHANGE MANAGEMENT

Solvency II is the most significant regulatory change intervention the insurance industry has ever experienced. On the external front, consultation activities are still underway with key issues being debated with gusto at industry forums across Europe and in Brussels. In the UK, the integration of part of the FSA into the Bank of England has spelt change for the Internal Model approval process with timelines brought forward, impacting programme contingency plans. On the internal front, programmes are ramping up their efforts to ensure a successful outcome, and for some, this activity is being carried out in tandem with other significant organizational change. Every level of the organization will be impacted in one way or another by the new regime. This places a requirement on the leadership team for strong people-change management skills.

5.1 AN EVOLVING WORKPLACE

The Solvency II regime will directly impact those who use capital in their day-to-day business. It could involve the restructuring of how the business is organized and, if so, it will have a significant impact on staff in these parts of the business. Across the organization, all are sure to be impacted by the culture transformation with the spotlight placed on risk-based decision-making. In addition, the Solvency II implementation programme itself will be a change initiative and, to ensure it is positioned to deliver, it is essential that the programme is treated as an extraordinary cross-business change programme and that existing initiatives are assessed and integrated to achieve synergies, minimize conflicts and ensure alignment with strategies. So Solvency II means change on a number of different levels. Some of these changes will be evolutionary and will be absorbed into everyday practices in a low-key manner. Other changes have the potential to be revolutionary and to turn people's worlds upside down. Leaders and line managers need to be alert to this reality and have a toolkit on hand for managing people through change.

5.1.1 The Change Readiness Assessment

A Change Readiness Assessment gathers information to establish how prepared individuals, teams and departments are to change in their organization. Typically, information is gathered from a target audience via a questionnaire and increasingly this is conducted online. A well-designed approach will gather information on topics such as:

- Leadership in the organization;
- Core purpose, strategies and goals;
- Employee engagement in strategic objectives;
- Change awareness;
- Job security;
- Learning opportunities.

When the approach used is sophisticated, data gathered can be measured against robust benchmarks and can be used in a variety of situations, such as:

- Acquisitions;
- Construction;
- Mergers; and
- Restructuring.

Data collated will be analysed and can provide:

- A clear indication of how prepared or 'ready' the focal organization is for change;
- Specific feedback and evidence on where the change management efforts need to be focused to ensure success;
- Highlights on the type and degree of change appreciated by employees;
- Specific intelligence on the transformational strengths and weaknesses of the focal organization.

Other benefits can include the following:

- Enables leaders to design and deliver bespoke oganizational design and development and change management solutions to areas of the business that need it most;
- Enables leaders to address the people factors that will both support and obstruct change;
- Informs decisions on people can be made before significant sums of money are invested;
- Establishes a robust benchmark for future reference.

In the Solvency II context, a Change Readiness Assessment will be particularly helpful in a merger and acquisition scenario or where a lot of contractors are hired and descend on BAU teams. The established workforce may well be hostile to the idea of contractors and consultants being brought in and may fear their jobs are under threat. They will have their own particular way of doing things and may have unions to represent their interests.

The assessment activity can also be customized and used with those external stakeholders whose support is considered critical as it will provide:

- Feedback on how ready different stakeholders are to change.
- Data on where support can be expected and alliances forged.
- Indications of where resistance can be expected and what the key issues are.

Of course, there is no guarantee that all stakeholder groups will wish to participate in this assessment exercise, but non-participation in itself will provide an indicator that this stakeholder group may need more attention.

5.1.2 The Buy-in Escalator

Securing stakeholder buy-in requires a staged approach. A key principle of the *buy-in escalator* is that the greater the degree of stakeholder understanding and involvement in the change process the greater the likelihood of their commitment to the change programme. This is true of all stakeholders, regardless of their profile.

This model illustrates that to secure the highest levels of commitment which is 'buy-in' (y-axis), it is first necessary to address the issues of 'awareness', 'understanding', and 'compliance' (x-axis). Each stage of this process can be addressed best through the use of specific strategies that will achieve particular objectives.

Figure 5.1   The stakeholder buy-in escalator

- To raise awareness – inform and be as transparent as is deemed prudent and ethical;
- To deepen understanding – educate, share the detail and answer questions;
- To get compliance – manage objections, address concerns and resolve issues, using confliction resolution techniques and forums where necessary;
- To get buy-in – involve stakeholders in key processes where possible.

No step of this process can be bypassed, but even then it cannot be assumed that stakeholder compliance and buy-in will be a given. For although stakeholders might be well informed about your programme, and although their understanding of what it entails may be excellent, your programme could be blocked in the early stage of consultation if stakeholders' understanding of proposals on the table leads them to reject them outright. This can happen when the required effort has not been put into addressing their concerns. To get stakeholders to at least comply with the direction of the programme, it is necessary to manage their objections and resolve their issues as they arise. Even then, there is still no guarantee that resistance will fully abate and make way for full stakeholder commitment. This is because to get real buy-in, stakeholders need to believe that they have had a genuine opportunity to shape that which affects them and protect their interests. From the outset, involve your stakeholders in key processes as soon as possible (in particular creative design and the decision-making processes) to help secure their buy-in.

5.1.3 Behaviour Mapping

While the aim with external stakeholders such as regulatory bodies will be to meet commitments and demonstrate compliance, internally the focus will be on driving behavioural change. It can be helpful, at the outset, to track where a stakeholder group is on the buy-in escalator and mark where they need to be. In the example below, the current state of each of the two stakeholders groups presented is marked with a '+' mark and their required state with an 'x'. This helps track the journey that needs to be taken with each group.

Table 5.1   Behavioural change: current state v. desired state

Stakeholder Group	Not Aware of SII	Aware	Understand	Compliant	Bought-in
Board			+		x
General Staff	+		x		

Then, one can define what each stakeholder group should do differently at the end of the journey.

Table 5.2   Required behavioural outcomes

	Behavioural outcome	What we want them to do differently
Boards and Committees		
Board Members	Commitment	I am committed to helping shape the Solvency II programme to deliver value for the business. I will demonstrate risk-based decision making and will meet all regulatory requirements.
Indirectly Impacted Staff		
General Employees	Compliance	I understand how Solvency II will impact the business and my role, and I will make risk-conscious decisions (as appropriate) to support the Solvency II regime.

5.1.4 The Change Curve

A well-known study by Kubler-Ross show that when people experience change (and grief in particular), they generally go through a series of phases as they come to terms with the change. As they move through the different stages, their attitude to the change and their ability to cope with it evolves as they develop strategies and experience a new way of living. The phases of this process are as follows:

- Shock and denial – when a person first receives bad news s/he can go into a state of denial or even shock. It may seem to people looking on that the person is coping well with the news but this can be far from the truth.
- Anger – as the person starts to understand the implications of the news on them they can enter into a state of anger and lash out at the world around them. This can impact people around them.
- Yearning for the 'good old days' – the next phase of this emotional process is for the person to try to bargain for the old way of doing things and to look back on the 'good old days' forgetting all the problems that were involved. As the reality of the change sinks in, a person can sink into a depression if they feel over whelmed by their loss and powerless in the face of it.
- Commitment to the new – but as they go about their day-to-day lives they start to experience a new way of living. With this comes acceptance and moving on.

This process is captured in Figure 5.2 which applies the research findings of Kubler-Ross to the business change context. On the x-axis time is represented, while on the y-axis positive and negative energy is represented. It will peak and dip over the course of the journey.

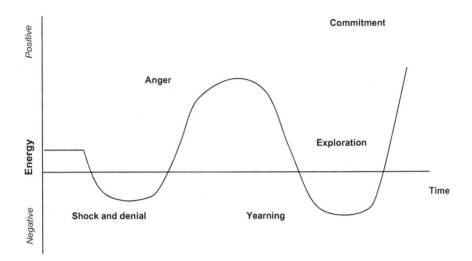

Figure 5.2   When change is bad news
Source: Gabrielle O'Donovan, *The Corporate Culture Handbook*, The Liffey Press, Ireland, 2006.

People are different and it is important to remember that individuals will move through the stages of the change curve at different speeds depending on how the change impacts them and the level of their own coping abilities. Line managers need to be alert to such differences on their teams and to treat people as individuals.

At each stage of the change curve, there are different strategies that the line manager can use:

- Shock and denial – prepare people by communicating that there is a problem early on. This gives them time to do a bit of scenario planning on potential future developments and take steps to protect their own interests. Also, don't package bad news as good. Be honest and transparent with people on the pros and cons of news being delivered.
- Anger – provide forums for people to raise their grievances and frustrations, encouraging a constructive note and positive energy. They may even find solutions to challenges faced and raise important questions. Allowing emotional processing will provide people with an outlet for their emotions and can re-channel potentially toxic energies constructively.
- Yearning and glamorizing of the 'good old days' – when people try to bargain for the old way of doing things it is important to remain firm. If they steadfastly refuse to let go of this phase, it may be that they need to be encouraged to move on to a new role and perhaps even a new organization.

When an individual appears to be falling into depression as they become overwhelmed with feelings of loss, give them one-to-one time and show an interest and concern for their issues. Set them goals for the future so that is where their focus and energies are directed. Offer the services of in-house counselling where it exists and make sure the person is getting the support they need to develop strategies to move on. For those who are showing signs of coming to terms with the change but who look back with 'rose coloured glasses' at how things were, support them by acknowledging the past but set them goals for the future. Communicate the benefits of the new set up and organize team-building activities where new teams are formed. Communicate wins and make sure people have the knowledge and skills they need to face the new world confidently.

- Commitment to the new – allow employees innovate and find new ways of doing thing so that they develop a sense of ownership for the new system. Promote those who champion the change and encourage them to be positive role-models. Once people learn that there are rewards to be reaped in the new world, they will be more embracing of the change.

5.1.5 Double-Loop Learning

Chris Argis (1980)[1] makes the case that effectiveness results from developing congruence between theory-in-use and theory-in-action; 'theory-in-use' is those beliefs and assumptions that guide our action, while 'espoused theory' is how we articulate what we do or think. Developing the desired congruence requires that we move beyond 'single loop learning' to double loop learning. Single loop learning involves, upon the detection of an error, the identification of another operational strategy that will work within the rules and boundaries of the original failed strategy. 'Double loop learning', on the other hand, involves critical reflection and the questioning of the rules and boundaries upon detection on an error. Argis believes that developing a double-loop approach to learning is critical to organizations and individuals facing change. It is an approach that can be built into centralized training programmes, on-the-job training and everyday practices.

5.1.6 Burke-Litwin Model

This model was created to examine organizational change and performance. It connects the assessment of the external and internal change context. The Burke-Litwin model makes the following key points:

- The external environment is the most powerful driver for organizational change.

---

1   C. Argis, *Knowledge for Action: A Guide to Overcoming Barriers to Organizational Change*, San Francisco, Jossey-Bass, 1993.

- Changes in the external environment lead to significant changes within an organization – the mission and strategy, its organizational culture and its leadership.
- Changes in these key factors lead to other changes within the organization – changes to structure, systems and management practices. These are more operational factors and changes in them may or may not have an organization-wide impact.
- Together these changes affect motivation, which in turn impacts on individual organizational performance.
- The model describes 12 organizational variables and the relationship between them. Each of the variables interacts and a change in any one of them can eventually impact on the others.

When data is gathered on each of the 12 variables and fed into a report for senior management, it can provide a useful frame of reference for understanding complex performance and change issues the organization is facing.[2]

5.1.7 Key Leadership Activities

According to a Prosci benchmarking report 'Best Practices in Change Management',[3] key leadership activities during the implementation phase of an enterprise wide change programme include the following:

- Communicate with direct reports about change, including information on why the change is happening, details about the change, expected impacts for the organization and the employer's job role, benefits of the change, answers to 'what's in it for me?';
- Demonstrate support for change; be role models and advocates for change in words and actions;
- Coach employees through the change process, encouraging them with positive support;
- Identify and manage resistance;
- Engage with and provide support to the project team, acting as liaison between impacted employees and the project and change teams.

During times of change when people are under duress, a friendly 'thank you' for a job well done can go a long way to support employee engagement and motivate the ranks. Also, establishing and maintaining an environment of trust is important and it keeps the ranks motivated and engaged. Members of the management team

---

2   See, www.interchange-resources.com.
3   Prosci Inc., Creasey, T. and Hiatt, J., *Best Practices in Change Management: 575 Organizations Share Lessons and Best Practices in Change Management*, Prosci benchmarking report, Loveland USA, 2012.

being visible and walking the shop floor to interact with staff can create a sense of 'being in this together' and reassure people that there is someone in-the-know at the helm, steering the ship. People need strong leadership in times of change and it is up to programme management and executive management to provide it.

5.2 COMMUNICATIONS AND CHANGE

Stakeholder Communications can facilitate culture transformation and effective change management. The stage you are at with a given stakeholder will determine what you can hope to achieve next, and this in turn will dictate which consultation channels are appropriate at any given time.

Consultation channels can be divided into two types – *information channels* and *engagement channels*.

- *Information channels* refer to largely one-way, non-participative interventions that are designed to share information. They are the standard fare of the more traditional communications department. In terms of influencing power, they have a 'push' effect. Use these primarily in the early stages of the process to raise awareness and increase understanding.
- *Engagement channels* refer to two-way interventions that require the active involvement and feedback of stakeholders. These have a 'pull' effect on stakeholders and draw the target audience to want to learn more about Solvency II. Use these to provide a forum for feedback, resolve issues, manage objections and involve stakeholders in key processes.

The following sections provide an inventory of some of the more relevant options that one can consider, together with advice on how they can be effectively used in the Solvency II context.

5.2.1 Information Channels

Booklets
Booklets can be used to explain widely to specific audiences the nature of Solvency II, its benefits and impact, key milestones, and so on. Key regulatory bodies and lobby groups already have their own online creations for downloading from their websites (for example, CEA). This media can also be used by Solvency II impacted organizations to communicate widely and internally, over-arching values and key messages that will support a risk management culture, the organizations risk appetite and what it means to the business. The beauty of the booklet as a tool is that it lends itself to straightforward messages and, when everyone gets their own copy, they can comfortably refer to it in their own time. While booklets might be seen as an unwelcome, additional cost during lean times, advances in

publishing software mean that it is possible to produce low-cost, high quality booklets in-house.

Briefings
To support wider communications, briefings can be used internally by line managers to update staff on Solvency II implementation progress against plans during the pre-implementation phase, how Solvency II will affect their part of the business and how it will affect how things are done locally. Line managers such get their input from a central point for example, the Stakeholder Communications Lead.

Communication packages
As part of a wider communication initiative, communication packages can be provided internally to line champions who will use the content to provide guidance to the troops. Package contents may include a combination of CDs, FAQ booklets, memory sticks and other materials.

Induction packages
Induction packages are a good channel for reaching employees, consultants and other contractors to brief them on Solvency II. Also, as many Solvency II teams are growing exponentially as the reality of the challenge posed by Solvency II implementation becomes apparent, remember to ensure newcomers to the team have a copy of the induction materials and that they are 'up to speed'.

Letters/emails
Letters and emails will be used a lot and in a variety of ways. For example, EU regulators and lobby groups use emails to distribute formal general memos (in this case the communication will generally be one-way and for information purposes only). Also, attendees at internal and external Solvency II related meetings use letters and email to follow up with other attendees to clarify on detail (in this case the communication is two way – or participative). A key point to note is that Solvency II regulator communications are being kept very formal and controlled for legal reasons with email being used more as a vehicle *to distribute* a PDF document (memo or letter) rather than as an alternative to a letter or memo itself.

Newsletters
Regular newsletters can provide the Solvency II programme team and internal stakeholders with updates such as progress against key milestones and stories about line wins. A visually appealing newsletter is more likely to be read, so include diagrams and photographs and break up large chunks of text into smaller digestible ones. When internal audiences are on different systems (as is often the case in a merger or acquisition) but all can access the intranet, host the newsletter on the intranet and distribute the link to it via email. Apart from

overcoming any access issues, this approach enables readership to be tracked. It also allows readers more control as they can click on those stories which most interest them.

Posters
Posters can be used in a variety of ways and are most effective when the emphasis is on the use of images rather or just a few words to rely key messages (these should be informed by the Stakeholder Communications Strategy). They are best used reach a large internal audience. Hard copy Solvency II posters can be positioned internally in staff cafeterias, offices, common rooms and public areas used by customers. Digital copies can be uploaded onto websites or placed on a memory stick in a communication package where one exists.

Presentations
Presentations usually form part of the agenda for internal meetings, workshops and roadshows, and external seminars and events. While they have become synonymous with 'PowerPoint™' slideshows, presentations can include video clips (embedded or otherwise), model displays and posters, and so on. In the Solvency II world, presentations feature largely for both internal and external communications as can be witnessed by a Google search.

Press releases
Press releases in newspapers and trade journals are the communication tool of choice to share strategically significant news with external audiences. For insurers and reinsurers, they can provide a general platform to promote wins (such as securing Solvency II compliance) and enhance the standing of the organization in the markets. In terms of protocols, press releases should always be prepared by the communications lead or programme manager, reviewed by the programme director and corporate communications, and approved by the steering committee before they are released.

Programme dashboard
A programme dashboard is a one-page summary which provides a snapshot update of programme status. It is divided into a number of sections such an executive summary, an overall RAG status, key milestones and key financial information. Apart from the executive summary, which will be in narrative form, the dashboard should not hold large chunks of text. Programme dashboards are a key component of Solvency II programme reporting because of the costs and level of resources involved.

Reports
Reports can be written to educate a specific audience on a particular Solvency II related issue and to inform the way forward. Reports can also be used as a basis for discussions and workshops to inform the way forward. A standard report will

state in the introduction section its purpose, who called for the report and who has been tasked with writing it. It will contain an executive summary, updates, research findings, conclusions and recommendations that will inform any future action. It will be written using an easy-to-read typeface and in an accessible format (A3-sized reports, printed in landscape and in a font size of just 10 points do not meet these criteria). But reports come in other formats and, in the Solvency II world, typical report formats include business cases, programme dashboards and detailed milestone reports.

Seminars
Currently, Solvency II seminars abound as specialists converge to learn about the latest research and practices. Where good progress is made with Solvency II implementation, it is appropriate to share such wins at external seminars to strengthen market confidence. As with any communications for external audiences, make sure that the content and key messages are signed off internally before it 'leaves the building'.

Surveys
An online survey can be used internally by the Stakeholder Communications team to establish a benchmark on staff awareness of Solvency II, its benefits and how it will impact the organization and the internal way of doing things. Post-implementation, this survey can be carried out once more with the same audience to get a measure on progress made.

Wallet cards
A wallet card is a small rectangular, laminated page that fits into a person's wallet. It may be one-sided or it may fold out, concertina like, to reveal hidden pages. A standard, one-sided, wallet card can be used to share the benefits of Solvency II and related core value statements that support a risk-management culture. The fold-out option can be used to share more detail, for example, the Three Pillar Model of the Lamfalussy Process. Experience has taught us to no longer include the every moving regime implementation timeline.

To summarize, while the channels mentioned above are typical 'push' channels that share information only, many can be used as tools to facilitate discussion in conjunction with the 'pull' channels and forums detailed below.

5.2.2 Engagement Channels

Bi-laterals
Bi-laterals are one-to-one meetings and can be used to consult with a stakeholder on the detail of a specific issue. They are often held for those stakeholders who have significant influence on the attainment of the programme objectives, as they afford a level of confidentiality that is not possible with other consultation

channels. Some stakeholders may be fearful of 'burning bridges' with their own constituencies and may feel unable to voice valid concerns in more open forums.

Conferences

Conferences are large-scale undertakings that are typically organized by professional event management teams. Solvency II conferences provide an excellent opportunity for directors and senior management to gather market intelligence on best practices, lessons learnt and latest developments.

Consultation documents

Formal Solvency II consultation documents include CEIOPS draft policy documents (or CPs) prepared for the EU to provide guidance on different aspects on Solvency II implementation. They are prepared by technical experts and are being used to facilitate discussions with focused groups of stakeholders. Every Solvency II programme team should have access to an online directory.

Focus groups

Focus groups are normally used for research purposes to explore the attitudes of specific target groups in relation to a specific issue. A small group that is a representative sample of a target audience will be invited to participate. In the focus group, a facilitator will conduct a guided discussion using open-ended questions as prompts. The process can be recorded and feedback will be collated and used to inform the organizer about next steps regarding the issue on the table. Focus groups can be used internally to solicit input on how practical and user-friendly new Solvency II measures are and how improvements can be made to the implementation process.

Meetings

Meetings are the backbone of stakeholder consultation. There are different types of meetings and each serves a particular purposes:

- *Face-to-face meetings* bring people together and they allow one the advantage of reading the body language that is going with the words of a given speaker. A round-table setting is best as it removes politics of 'who is sitting next to whom?'
- *Conference calls* are useful where attendees are spread geographically across different time zones. They are best suited for dealing with internal audiences and where those parties participating have already met in person and established a rapport. While they do serve a purpose, it is often the casual conversation one has with other participants directly after a face-to-face meeting that provides the most useful insights into some of the real issues and agenda so, where possible, take the time and effort to meet key stakeholders face-to-face.
- *Meetings with external organizations and groups* provide Solvency II impacted organizations the opportunity to ask key experts for clarification on

issues. They may be organized by special interest groups, or by government agencies in line with their statutory commitments.

We have all heard the story about the organization which banned all meetings as they were considered a waste of resources. To me, this is over-zealous and an example of 'throwing the baby out with the bathwater'. Meetings are the backbone of any consultation process as they can be used to raise awareness, improve understanding, get compliance and secure stakeholder buy-in. The important thing is to ensure that meetings are conducted properly. In a well-organized meeting, a meeting Terms of Reference has been established, the right people are in attendance, all were advised in a timely manner that the meeting will be held, the agenda is distributed in advance, and minutes are taken and distributed shortly after. During the meeting, everyone is given a chance to speak, ask questions, and all are treated in a respectful manner and no one personality should dominate proceedings.

Question and answer sessions (Q&As)
Q&A sessions provide stakeholders with an opportunity to ask clarifying questions, get feedback, deepen their understanding and make informed decisions:

- *Live Q&A sessions* that are hosted by senior programme executives can provide the best value for their audience as they afford the opportunity to get the story 'straight from the horse's mouth' and allow for immediate feedback. Such sessions draw people together and remove barriers between groups, but they can go wrong when the speaker does not handle a question well. To manage this, the Q&A session organizer should ensure that the speaker/s is well prepped in terms of who is in the audience, what the 'hot topics' are and any frequently asked questions. The speaker should do their homework and come well prepared. Live Q&A sessions should form part of the agenda for Solvency II programme team town halls.
- *Online Q&As* can have the same benefits, but particular care should be taken to ensure that when the request is put out for questions, the audience should be allowed some time to digest information given and prepare their questions. Westerners are less comfortable with quiet spaces and may be quick to jump in and fill the quiet when global audiences would prefer some time to mull and consider before they raise their questions.
- *Web-based online Q&A forums* are useful when it is simply impractical to gather together the target audience because of the sheer numbers, or geographical challenges. Questions can be posted anonymously with the forum managed by an administrator and governed by a clear policy on how to use the forum.

Q&A sessions can be used in conjunction with one-way communication channels such as seminars to encourage audience participation.

Roadshows

A roadshow is a useful way to reach target audiences who otherwise might be difficult to reach. This may be due to their geographical location or some other constraints. With a roadshow, a touring core team can visit stakeholders to present them with a travelling exhibition, presentations and workshops. This may be conducted at the very outset, to secure investors and sponsors, or it may be conducted further down the line to reach chambers of commerce and other industry stakeholders. A key benefit of roadshows is that they can garner support in areas that it is difficult to secure, but they can be a costly exercise given the travelling expenses that will be run up.

Workshops

Workshops are suitable for problem-solving purposes with participants carefully chosen to represent a specific group. Clear inputs and required outputs are determined upfront and participants must work together on the problem in hand to find possible solutions. For credibility purposes, and to leverage off any buy-in achieved with the group, the workshop organizer should prepare a post-workshop write up on the process and outputs and circulate this amongst participants and any commitments entered into with the group should be upheld. Workshops demand the active participation of attendees to create output and are not to be confused with seminars.

Website

While company websites (extranet and intranet) did start off as one-way information channels, the evolution on online communication tools has led to the advent of participation channels such as blogs and online Q&A forums which, when well designed, can have a strong 'pull' influence on intended audiences.

Extranet

The key objective of the programme website should be to act a portal to general information for the community at large, with links directing users to more detailed information. Extranets are more suitable for targeting the general public and less so for specific audiences who may have conflicting needs and agendas.

Intranet

A programme intranet site should focus on the interests and needs of the workforce. These pages will become the chief interface for those interested in a quick and easy understanding of the programme. Consultation materials (such as newsletters, consultation brochures, route maps, information sheets and market research results) can be uploaded to the site for easy access. Beware that even communications intended for internal parties only could well end up in the hands of the media, so careful consideration should be given to all content before it is uploaded and released into the public domain.

Both extranets and intranets must be regularly updated if they are to maintain their audiences.

This is not a definitive summary of communication channels but it by now it should be quite apparent that different channels will serve different purposes but can be used in conjunction with each other. For this reason, we now need to consider the various options within the context of what level of stakeholder support we are trying to achieve with a particular group.

5.2.3 Channel Mix and Impact

How we use and mix communication channels will have an effect on a stakeholder's stance as illustrated in Figure 5.3.

For example:

- The low use of both information channels and engagement channels will result in a majority of 'drifters' – those who have limited understanding of the programme and little buy-in to it.
- The low use of information channels mixed with a high use of engagement channels will result in a majority of 'wild cards' – those who forge ahead with probably the best intentions but with little understanding of the bigger picture.

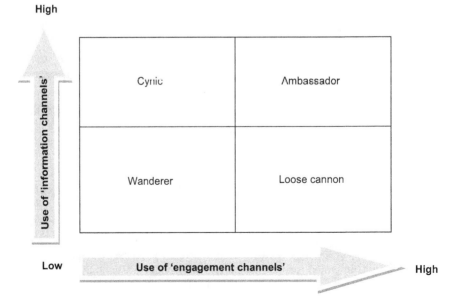

Figure 5.3   Reactions to channel mix

- The high use of information channels mixed with a low use of engagement channels will result in a majority of 'cynics' – those who considered themselves very knowledgeable about the programme but talk about it in a disparaging way.
- The high use of both information channels and engagement channels will create champions who will promote programme values and messages.

5.3 CHAPTER SUMMARY

Solvency II will mean change for the organization on a number of different levels. Some of these changes will be evolutionary and will be absorbed into everyday practices in a low-key manner. Other changes have the potential to be revolutionary and to turn people's worlds upside down. Leaders and line managers need to be alert to this reality and have a toolkit on hand for managing people through change.

To maximize stakeholder support it is necessary to guide each of your stakeholder groups through a process which is depicted in the *Buy-in Escalator* model. This model illustrates that to secure the highest levels of stakeholder buy-in it is necessary to address the issues of stakeholder awareness, understanding and compliance in a step-by-step fashion. Different consultation channels will help address each of these stages.

Consultation channels can be divided into *information channels*, which are largely one-way, and *engagement channels* that require the active involvement of stakeholders. The former includes interventions such as press releases, booklets, newsletters and leaflets while the latter encompasses meetings, focus groups, events, workshops and site visits. Info channels will have a 'push' effect on their target audience while participation channels will have a 'pull' effect. The communications channel mix will achieve different results with stakeholders, creating either 'cynics', 'wanderers', 'loose cannons' or 'champions' of the cause. Be sure to review plans carefully, to get the best mix.

CHAPTER 6

STAKEHOLDER ANALYSIS

While earlier efforts to manage stakeholders will have focused primarily on keeping the regulator happy and influencing Solvency II developments via industry lobby groups, a broad range of organizational stakeholders will be impacted by the new regime. To manage these stakeholders most effectively, formal stakeholder management activities are recommended:

- *Identification* – name stakeholders;
- *Profiling* – gain insights based on stakeholders' strategic objectives and key attributes, for example, level of power to influence organization or initiative, and the nature of their interests or stake in the same, in order to predict their behaviour and develop appropriate strategies for managing them;
- *Prioritization* – based on profiles, rank stakeholders according to how integral they are to the organization (or initiative) achieving its objectives so as to determine how stakeholders should be involved in consultation processes, and how resources should be allocated to match their different profiles.

These activities and their outputs help programme management determine where best to place resources and how best to manage stakeholders. Here, various models are put forward which offer alternative ways of approaching these activities.

6.1 STAKEHOLDER IDENTIFICATION

In Chapter 3 we considered the stakeholder challenge posed by Solvency II and learnt about different stakeholders. These can be presented in lists or, for visual learners, using an image such as the Stakeholder Snapshot.

6.1.1 The Stakeholder Snapshot

The Stakeholder Snapshot can present a multitude of stakeholders in one single image which clusters stakeholders in a particular way; for example, according to the nature of their business. Such an image makes it very easy for a manager to understand the big picture and where a particular stakeholder fits into it. It also makes it much easier, during this initial stakeholder identification stage, to identify missing stakeholders that have yet to be considered. In the Solvency II context, it is useful to cluster stakeholders in the following groups and subgroups:

- External – Regulators, Lobby Groups, The Markets and Special Interest Groups (SIGs);
- Internal – Governance, Committees, Directly Impacted Teams, Indirectly Impacted Teams.

In Figure 6.1, external stakeholders are on the left, and internal stakeholders are on the right. Solvency II programme management will have direct dealings with all internal stakeholders, and some external stakeholders such as regulatory groups and lobby groups that they are aligned to.

6.2 STAKEHOLDER PROFILING

Once stakeholders have been identified, it is possible to profile them. Fundamental to that process is developing an understanding of how Solvency II will affect the different groups.

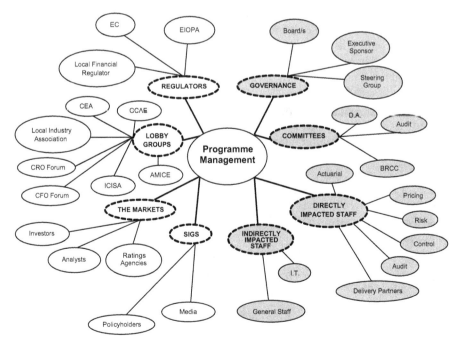

Figure 6.1   Solvency II programme stakeholders

6.2.1 Stakeholder Impacts

Stakeholders will be impacted by the Solvency II regime, and individual implementation programmes, in a variety of ways. Here, we identify some of those key impacts, taking each programme stakeholder group in turn.

Table 6.1   External stakeholders

Regulators	Impacts
European Commission (on behalf of the European Parliament)	The European Commission is tasked with successfully implementing Solvency II across EU states by 1 January 2016. The Commission will not be impacted by individual Solvency II implementation programmes and will receive reports on overall developments from EIOPA. The Commission will, however, liaise directly with individual entities in response to any lobbying activity from such entities.
EIOPA	EIOPA is tasked with supervising successful delivery on behalf of the European Commission. Again, EIOPA will not concern itself with individual Solvency II implementation programmes and will receive reports on overall developments from local country regulators. EIOPA will, however, interact with individual entities that approach EIOPA to lobby on issues.
Local country regulator	Local country regulators are tasked with supervising affected entities through the Solvency II implementation process. Local regulators will deal directly with affected entities and will want to see clear plans that are delivered against in a timely and effective way. Local country regulators' plans and resources will be impacted, to some extent, by how individual programmes evolve.

The Markets	Impacts
Investors	Investors will be concerned with changes in return on capital due to the new prudential regime. They should also be happy that economic capital and regulatory capital will be better aligned, as a result of Solvency II, meaning investors and regulators will have some worldview and speak the same language.
Analysts	Analysts will not be directly impacted by individual programmes. However, individual company performance during Solvency II implementation and beyond will have a bearing on analysts' reports, influencing public perceptions, and so these stakeholders need to be treated with respect.
Ratings Agencies	Company performance during Solvency II implementation and beyond will have a bearing on agencies' ratings for individual entities.

Table 6.1   External stakeholders *(concluded)*

Lobby Groups	Impacts
CEA GCAE CRO Forum CFO Forum ICISA AMICE Local industry associations	Lobby groups are responsible for promoting the interests of their members. They will not be concerned with individual Solvency II implementation programmes, but in the views of its members regarding Solvency II consultation papers in particular and key issues therein.

Special Interest Groups	Impacts
Policyholders/ Customers	Solvency II is ultimately for the protection of policyholders. If an organization's risk appetite changes significantly as a result of Solvency II, customers will need to know. Products carry specific risk appetites and if any such risk appetite changes it could affect the products on offer and the pricing of those products. In theory, policyholders will also need to be informed of any changes to policy terminology resulting from Solvency II, though no such changes are envisaged.
The Media	Media groups have an interest in the progress of an organization with Solvency II compliance only in terms of how newsworthy any developments are. Media groups can influence the brand image and reputation of any given organization and so need to be managed accordingly.

Table 6.2   Internal stakeholders

Governance	Impacts
The Board/s	Solvency II requires the Board to demonstrate risk-based decision-making, and this ability will be tested by local regulators as part of the Solvency II compliance process. The Board will also need to demonstrate that a risk culture has been embedded and that Solvency II standards of governance and operation are in effect.
Executive Sponsor	The onus is on the programme Executive Sponsor to oversee the successful implementation of Solvency II. For some, this can amount to driving major organization-wide change in addition to BAU activity.
Steering Group	The programme Steering Group is responsible for driving the successful implementation of Solvency II on behalf of the Executive Sponsor, in addition to running their day-to-day BAU activities.

Committees	Impacts
Design Authority	The programme Design Authority will need to make right decisions on road to Solvency II compliance, and to demonstrate due process and due consideration of issues in relation to business strategies.
Audit Committee	The Audit Committee will need to keep independent oversight of Solvency II implementation.
BRCC	The BRCC will need to review Solvency II related issues prior to their going to the Board, with a view to making decisions on behalf of the Board.

Directly Impacted Staff	Impacts
Risk Management Function	A Risk Management function will need to be established where one doesn't exist and a Chief Risk Officer will need to be appointed where there is none. The risk function will need to be overseen by the Board or an executive director. Any such reorganization will directly impact staff; there will be winners and losers. An already established risk function will need to align current policies, practices etc. with the Solvency II requirement and this includes the embedding of a risk culture that measures up to Solvency II.
Actuarial Function	Solvency II will mean a shift from the 'Responsible Actuary' or 'Actuarial Function Holder' role in operation in many EU member states prior to Solvency II. Where none exists, an Actuarial function will need to be established. Again, any such reorganization will directly impact staff; there will be winners and losers.
Internal Control and Compliance Function	Where Internal Control and Compliance is currently integrated with another function, it must be separated. Any such reorganization will directly impact staff and the change will mean different things to different people. The new requirements as laid out in the Directive will change how things are done internally and this in turn will change what is required of Control and Compliance.
Internal Audit	Solvency II requires the establishment of an Internal Audit function where one doesn't exist. This function must be independent and cannot be combined with risk and compliance. Any such reorganization will directly impact staff.
Pricing	Solvency II will mean a change in how capital is calculated and this will directly impact the product portfolio and the pricing of products. The strategy and pricing teams will need to work with programme management to understand what this means in their own organization.
Delivery Partners	Solvency II will impact delivery partners to varying degrees depending on where their skill set lies. The immediate impact on BAU teams involved in implementing Solvency II could be such that they are managing their own team in the business and also a Solvency II implementation team. Further down the line Solvency II will mean a significantly new way of doing things for some, such as those involved in reporting to the Regulator.

Table 6.2   Internal stakeholders *(concluded)*

Indirectly Impacted Staff	Impacts
General Staff	While only certain groups of staff will be directly impacted by Solvency II, all will be indirectly impacted at least by the embedding of a risk culture that lives up to the Solvency II standard. For general staff this will mean a shift in their operating beliefs, assumptions and values in relation to their relationship with risk and other related areas. All staff will be responsible for being risk-conscious in their day-to-day activities, and will be measured accordingly.
IT	Where the organization goes down the Internal Model route, Solvency II will appear on the CIO agenda as the company considers how they will feed their Internal Model to ensure complete and accurate data. This may require an investment in risk-modelling and capital-aggregation tools to address the quantitative requirements and other kinds of data that may include market risk, regulatory risk and even operational risk. IT may be required to align IT architecture, enable advanced IT risk management tools and treat data as a strategic asset.

Understanding how stakeholders are impacted by Solvency II will help one develop an understanding of what their stake or interest/s will be.

6.2.2 Stakeholder Mapping

Stakeholder mapping is a useful tool for analysing the political context in which strategies are developed (Johnson and Scholes, 2001).[1] Different techniques are outlined below.

Power and Interest Grids
According to Bryson et al. (2002)[2] 'Power versus Interest Grids' are very helpful for identifying stakeholder coalitions which should or should not be encouraged. They highlight whose buy-in *must* be secured and provide data that can be helpful in convincing certain stakeholders to change their stance. They also help determine which stakeholders' power bases and interests must be taken into account in order to address a given issue.

---

1   G. Johnson and K. Scholes (eds), *Exploring Public Strategy*, Pearson Education, Harlow, UK, 2001.
2   J. Bryson, G. Cunningham and K. Lokkesmoe, What to Do When Stakeholders Matter: The Case of Problem Formulation for the African American Men Project of Hennepin Country Minnesota, *Public Administration Review*, 2002, 62:5, 568–84.

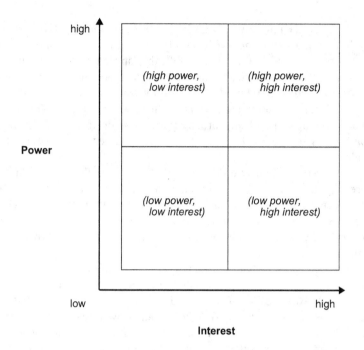

Power

low

(high power,
low interest)

(high power,
high interest)

(low power,
low interest)

(low power,
high interest)

low   high

Interest

Figure 6.2   Classic Stakeholder Power/Interest Grid

A Power versus Interest Grid is generally a 2 × 2 matrix where the size of a stakeholders' interest is depicted on the x-axis (how much they have invested), while their power (to influence the organization's strategic goals) is depicted on the y-axis. Depending on where they are plotted on the four quadrants of the grid, a stakeholder's profile can be classified as *High Power, High Interest*; *High Power, Low Interest*; *Low Power, High Interest* or *Low Power, Low Interest*. Then, based on where they are positioned on the grid, each stakeholder group can be considered in turn to determine their power and interest, relative to each other.

- In the original model of Freeman and Reed (1983),[3] the first dimension is one of 'interest' or 'stake' and ranges from an equity interest to an economic or marketplace interest, to a 'kibitzer' or 'influencer' stake. The second dimension is a stakeholders' economic and political power.
- In the Mendelow version (1991),[4] and depending on where they are plotted on the four quadrants of the grid, stakeholders can be classified

---

3   R.E. Freeman and D.L. Reed, Stockholders and Stakeholders: A New Perspective on Stakeholder Governance, *California Management Review*, 1983, 25:3, 83–94.

4   A. Mendelow, *Proceedings of the 2nd International Conference on Information Systems*, Cambridge, MA, 1991.

as *Key Players* (High Power, High Interest), *Keep Satisfied* (High Power, Low Interest), *Keep Informed* (Low Power, High Interest) and *Minimal Effort* (Low Power, Low Interest). With this approach, Mendelow make steps towards defining broad strategies for engagement (*'Keep Satisfied'* and *'Keep Informed'*) but doesn't follow through for the other two groups; one classification simply labels the stakeholder as a *'Key Player'* without making explicit any broad strategy, while the fourth *'Minimal Effort'* refers to the level of effort to expend rather than a strategy for engagement.

- In their version, Eden and Akerman (1998)[5] state that, depending on where they are plotted on the four quadrants of the grid and their resulting profiles (cf. Figure 1.2), stakeholders can be classified as *Players* (High Power, High Interest), *Context Setters* (High Power, Low Interest), *Subjects* (Low Power, High Interest) and the *Crowd* (Low Power, Low Interest).

- A more useful and widely used tool is a refinement of the Mendelow model (source unknown). It is more consistent, defining four broad strategies for engagement; *Manage Closely* (High Power, High Interest), *Keep Satisfied* (High Power, Low Interest), *Keep Informed* (Low Power, High Interest) or simply *Monitor* (Low Power, Low Interest). An advantage of this adapted model over the others is that it consistently recommends practical strategies for managing stakeholders differently, based on their unique profiles (see Figure 6.2).

In Figure 6.3, it is demonstrated how some Solvency II regulator stakeholders might appear on the Stakeholder Grid during the implementation phase.

The relationship with the local regulatory is of paramount importance and will need to be managed closely. EIOPA and the European Commission, on the other hand, are not concerned with individual implementation programmes and so have a low stake in such programmes, but they do have a lot of power over proceedings and so they need to be kept satisfied during any interactions with a given organization over, for example, lobbying issues.

Stakeholder Influence Diagrams (also known as Integrated Power/Interest Grids)
Stakeholder Influence Diagrams are based on Power versus Interest Grids. Taking a completed grid that has stakeholders plotted on it, one can proceed to trace the lines of influence that flow between different parties. Sometimes these will be one-way while in other instances they will be two way. The output of this exercise provides more valuable pieces of the collage.

---

5   C. Eden and F. Akerman, *Making Strategy: The Journey of Strategic Management*, London, Sage Publications, 1998.

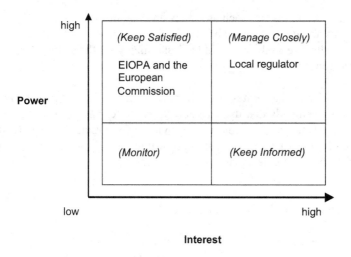

Power

(Keep Satisfied)	(Manage Closely)
EIOPA and the European Commission	Local regulator
(Monitor)	(Keep Informed)

low   high

Interest

Figure 6.3   Solvency II Regulatory Stakeholder Grid

The Power, Urgency and Legitimacy Diagram
According to Mitchell et al. (1997),[6] a third way of profiling stakeholders is in terms of three attributes; power, urgency and legitimacy. They put forward a seven-part typology based on assessments of the strengths of these three attributes and proposed that the various classes of stakeholders might be identified based on the possession of one, two or all three of the attributes. Stakeholders who show only one of the three characteristics are defined as 'Latent Stakeholders'. Stakeholders who show two out of three characteristics are defined as 'Expectant Stakeholders', while those who show all three attributes are 'Definitive Stakeholders'. In this model, the new variable is 'urgency' and this expresses how quickly this stakeholder needs to be dealt with in order to offset any risk posed. Urgency is dynamic in nature and will be closely tied to specific stakeholder issues.

Although the benefits of conducting stakeholder analysis would seem obvious, quite often they are not conducted. In 'What to do When Stakeholders Matter: A Guide to Stakeholder Identification and Analysis Techniques' (2003), J.M. Bryson identified reasons why people do not conduct stakeholder analysis:

• The state of prior knowledge; lack of understanding of the process leads to fear of incompetence being exposed or, alternatively, overconfidence about the knowledge held about stakeholders leads to closed-mindedness;

---

6   R.K. Mitchell, B.R. Agle and D.J. Wood, Towards a Theory of Stakeholder Identification and Salience: Defining the Principle of the Who and What Really Counts, *Academy of Management Review*, October, 1997, 22:4, 53–886.

- Resource-related issues such as money and manpower;
- Concerns about what the analyses would reveal;
- Concern that the analyses might be destabilizing (to the status quo);
- Ethical concerns.

Bryson believes that what unites these reasons seems to be an underlying fear or worry. He recommends that these reasons are counter-balanced by arguments for doing the analyses, namely that they provide information that is potentially extremely valuable in creating and sustaining winning coalitions and ensuring the long-term viability of policies, plans and programmes.

6.3 STAKEHOLDER PRIORITIZATION

Based on their emerging profiles, stakeholders can now be classified and prioritized to determine where the focus and energies of managers should be, and how resources should be allocated. An equitable approach is recommended; those who are to be managed closely will get more attention and resources directed at them while, at the other end of the spectrum, those who are to be simply monitored will get the least.

6.4 CHAPTER SUMMARY

Stakeholder analysis allows us to develop a more sophisticated understanding of who are stakeholders are and this, in turn, informs the amount of resources we should expend on them. It involves three steps: stakeholder identification, stakeholder profiling and stakeholder prioritization.

Stakeholder identification involves capturing all constituents on the radar, and perhaps illustrating the stakeholder community in a single snapshot. The 'Power versus Interest Grid' allows us to plot a stakeholder's power and interest. This tool defines the broad strategies for engagement based on which quadrant a stakeholder sits; strategies include 'manage closely', 'keep satisfied', 'keep informed' or 'monitor' and will, in turn, dictate where resources should be allocated. Another approach involves assessing a stakeholder's influence, commitment (to their interests) and potential impact on the programme if they pursue their interests. Alternatively, the 'legitimacy of links' test enables us to identify authentic stakeholders who have formal and defined links with the programme, and false stakeholders who do not. Based on emerging profiles, stakeholders can be prioritized and programme resources allocated equitably.

CHAPTER 7

THE STAKEHOLDER COMMUNICATIONS STRATEGY

Strategies steer day-to-day implementation plans and, for better or for worse, determine outcomes and results. Therefore, this chapter is wholly concerned with the development of a *practical* Stakeholder Communications strategy which supports the organization's efforts to achieve Solvency II compliance, a goal which can in turn enable new and market relevant corporate strategies.

While the requirement to secure Solvency II compliance status will be a given for all, for some the connection between corporate strategies and achieving Solvency II compliance is not so clear with any implementation programme perceived as an operational level response to fill a need created by external regulatory pressures. But is this an adequate assessment? To answer the question we need to go back to 2002 when Solvency II was first conceived and consider how industry responses have varied – as illustrated in Chapter 2.

Affected entities with strong strategic management capabilities have worked proactively to understand potential impacts on the industry as a whole and on their given organization. This has set the agenda for their industry lobbying activity, allowing them to shape the debate around the final content of the EU Directive and further guidance measures. It has also helped them to develop a picture of the evolving environmental context, and informed strategic planning sessions and strategy assessment activities also. Strategy assessment methodologies will have included benchmarking, scenario planning, shareholder value analysis, core competency analysis and time-based competition. The outputs of such activities may have led to:

- The reconfirmation of an existing customer-focused strategy (such as the 'Treating Customers Fairly' strategy adopted as a regulatory requirement by all UK financial institutions);
- The creation of new pricing strategies (as mentioned previously, many investment guarantees are expected to become more expensive);
- Changes to individual product strategies and product portfolio strategies to reap risk diversification benefits;

- Changes to any diversification strategies (Solvency II will result in changes to the financial position of an entity which will add to or detract from existing diversification benefits);
- The retiming of M&A strategies where an imminent merger may load excessive risk onto the existing Solvency II implementation programme in the run up to 1 January 2016.

Those organizations with weaker strategic management capabilities will have been more tactical in their response to the regime change, seeking merely to secure compliance status and without a line of sight of the longer term game. Because their Solvency II implementation programme has little bearing on strategic planning processes, such organizations are not best placed to evolve with the external environment and this will impact their ability to remain competitive in a Solvency II world. And then there are those who fall in the middle – organizations which adopted a 'compliance mindset' in the earlier phases of Solvency II and which are now working on aligning the implementation programme with business strategies. The level of response chosen by a given organization will determine the organization's readiness for the Solvency II world, post 'Go Live'. This is captured in Figure 7.1.

To summarize, any given Solvency II implementation programme is best placed if it has a direct relationship with corporate strategies. Such an approach supports the organization's efforts to adapt to an evolving environment. Also, by framing Solvency II as a strategy enabler, support can be garnered across the business, making it in the interests of key business leaders to clear the path of obstacles and support programme delivery.

A Solvency II Stakeholder Communications strategy is a document which can be used by management to outline the planned approach to maximize programme stakeholder support and meet agreed goals. It can also serve to illustrate how programme management networks and interacts with audiences – a process which is iterative and evolving in nature. The strategy will have a cross-functional impact with its reach extending to external stakeholders. Key features of the strategy design include the following:

1. Introduction
2. Principles, goals and objectives
3. Audiences and stakeholder management
4. Key messages
5. Branding
6. Consultation and communications planning
7. Programme stakeholder reporting
8. Risks, assumptions, issues and dependencies
9. Resourcing
10. Key measures

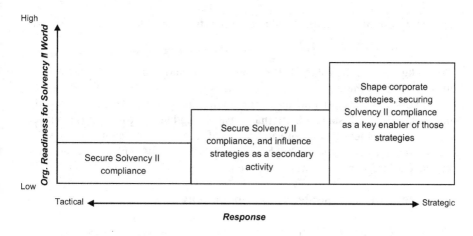

Figure 7.1   Responses to Solvency II: tactical to strategic

Each section herein describes each of these elements, containing practical guidance plus useful tools and templates which can be customized to suit the needs of individual organizations. Where necessary, elaboration is provided for the benefit of those entrusted with the development of the Stakeholder Communications strategy to highlight potential challenges and solutions. The actual strategy document presented to senior executives for discussion and eventual sign off would distil the key points developed in the different sections of this chapter, and be presented together with supporting evidence such as stakeholder profiling activity outputs and a Risk Log (cf. p. 112). The format chosen to present the strategy document should suit the culture of the given organization and, based on current industry trends, is most likely to be a Word™ document and/or a PowerPoint™ deck.

7.1 INTRODUCTION

The introductory section of the strategy document can contain a background section, a scoping of 'Stakeholder Communications' to define the context, a review of activity to date, a brief description of research methodology and a framing of the Stakeholder Communications challenge.

7.1.1 Background

This section will describe the general business context and identify the business opportunity. This will include a reference to the environmental forces (regulatory) which are driving the implementation programme and also a high-level reference to how the organization can also take advantage of any opportunities. For example, in the UK, Solvency II builds on the ICA regime introduced by the FSA at the end of 2004. It also provides the stimulus and opportunity to enhance existing risk and capital management practices.

The background section should also reference any merger or acquisition where the other entity is in the insurance industry and where this may mean the integration of two Solvency II programme teams for the firm in question. Depending on which model is being used (standard, internal or partial) and how the merger is managed, such an arrangement could raise the risk profile of the programme, the level of change management interventions required to successfully implement change and the Stakeholder Communications requirement.

7.1.2 Scope of Stakeholder Communications

The term 'Stakeholder Communications' can mean different things to different people. For the purposes of this book, 'Stakeholder Communications' encompasses stakeholder management, stakeholder educational programmes, internal communications and external communications. In the Solvency II world, it also includes the programme stakeholder reporting process because this is a core part of Stakeholder Communications. Therefore, the Stakeholder Communications workstream is likely to be directly responsible for:

- Stakeholder management planning and governance;
- Solvency II programme stakeholder reporting planning and governance;
- Stakeholder education programmes, for example Solvency II Board training and Solvency II Induction training;
- Internal communications planning and delivery;
- External communications planning and delivery.

Through its activities, this workstream will support people change management (helping people through change). Also, it will support the embedding of a risk management culture.

7.1.3 Review and Findings

The review section will summarize how Stakeholder Communications have been conducted in the past, with 'the past' referring to earlier stages of the Solvency II programme and to other relevant processes and practices. The review will be based on a structured gap-analysis that also considers how stakeholders perceive the organization and any gaps that need to be filled to meet strategic objectives. For example, the assessment may show that, to date, communications with stakeholders have been one-way with little opportunity for dialogue and this may be due to a lack of suitable manpower to resource Stakeholder Communications. Findings may also reflect an internally focused or 'naval gazing' approach with little or no interactions with external stakeholders, beyond regulators and lobby groups. This section can also identify key touchpoints which the Stakeholder Communications team will interact with across the organization in the course of their duties, for example, the Solvency II Steering Committee, internal communications, external communications, learning and development and human resources. Where such interaction is new to either party, it may be necessary to agree the processes governing the interaction.

Also, those reviewing the strategy document will want to know what steps have been taken to understand the organization's requirement and, specifically, how data has been collated. A savvy reader would expect to see evidence of varied methodologies, for example:

- Visits to key branches/offices;
- Interviews with key stakeholders such as the Executive Sponsor, members of the Steering Committee and those requesting regular stakeholder reports;
- Surveys to gather stakeholder input;
- Desk research of historical practices;
- Observation in the workplace of everyday practices.

Gathering data from a variety of sources will make it possible to establish a baseline which can be used for later measurement activities. Such groundwork adds substance to findings and proposals.

7.1.4 Framing the Challenge

At the highest level, the Stakeholder Communications challenge is framed by the EU Directive and supporting material such as the draft Level 2 measures and Level 3 Supervisory Guidance. The Directive was finalized and endorsed in May 2009 while Level 2 guidance was finalized in 2012. Key relevant articles therein include the following:

Table 7.1   Solvency II Stakeholder Communications and the EU Directive

EU Directive	
Responsibility of the Administrative or Management Body – Article 40	Member states shall ensure that the administrative, management or supervisory body of the insurance or reinsurance undertaking has the ultimate responsibility for the compliance by the undertaking with the laws, regulation and administrative provisions adopted pursuant to this Directive.
Fit and Proper Requirements – Article 42	Insurance and reinsurance undertakings shall ensure that all persons who effectively run the undertaking or have other key functions meet, at all times, the following requirements: a. their professional qualifications, knowledge and experience are adequate and enable sound and prudent management (fit); b. they are of good repute and integrity (proper).

Table 7.1   Solvency II Stakeholder Communications and the EU Directive *(concluded)*

EU Directive	
Risk Management – Article 43	Insurance and reinsurance undertakings shall have in place an effective risk management system comprising strategies, processes and reporting procedures necessary to identify, measure, monitor, manage and report, on a continuous basis the risks, at an individual and at an aggregated level, to which they are or could be exposed, and their interdependencies.

Level 2 Draft Regulation	
General Governance Requirements – Article 249 SG1; Article 41 (1) of the Directive	Insurance and reinsurance undertakings shall have in place a system of governance which complies with at least, the following: • to establish, implement and maintain effective cooperation, internal reporting and communication of information at all relevant levels of the undertaking.
Internal Control System – Article 257 SG5; Article 46 (1) of the Directive	Insurance and reinsurance undertakings shall have in place an appropriate culture and environment that supports effective internal control activities, effective information and communication procedures and adequate monitoring mechanisms.
Fit to the Business – Article 212 TSIM2; Article 120 of the Directive	Insurance and reinsurance undertakings shall ensure that the design of the Internal Model is aligned with their business and shall ensure that at least: • the modelling approaches reflect the nature, scale and complexity of the risks inherent in the business of the insurance or reinsurance undertaking; • the outputs of the Internal Model and the content of the internal and external reporting of the insurance or reinsurance undertaking are consistent; • the outputs of the Internal Model and the content of the internal and external reporting of the insurance or reinsurance undertaking are consistent.
Internal Model Technical Provisions *[IM4]*	The procedure to be followed for the approval of an Internal Model envisages on-going communication between the supervisory authorities and the insurance or reinsurance undertaking. It is best practice for communication to begin before the formal application is submitted to the supervisory authorities. Communication between the supervisory authorities and the insurance or reinsurance undertaking should continue throughout the assessment of the application and after the Internal Model is approved through the supervisory review process.

Note: As outlined in Chapter 4, additional Articles will be relevant to the culture component of the new solvency regime.

The supporting 'Level 3 Supervisory Guidance' is currently under development and is not expected to be finalized any time soon, but in the draft guidance published pre-consultation, Guideline 6 (TSIM3) states the following requirement which has significant implications for the Stakeholder Communications workstream:

> *Undertakings may provide training, seminars, induction programmes or workshops on the Internal Model to management and staff using the Internal Model for decision-making. The supervisors may use interviews of senior management and ask detailed questions to persons responsible within an undertaking to assess the understanding of the Internal Model. The supervisors may also review the documentation of the minutes of the board meetings or appropriate decision-making bodies to assess compliance with the use test.[1]*

7.2 GOALS AND OBJECTIVES

Aligning goals and objectives can help ensure that the different communities in the workforce are working to the same drumbeat and speaking the same language. Such alignment can be achieved via a cascade effect. It can help ensure that any programme support strategies (such as this one) are organizing activities in line with programme goals and objectives.

7.2.1 Programme Goals and Objectives

Programme goals and objectives will be shaped by the EU Directive and business strategies. Examples are given below:

- Achieve Solvency II compliance by 1 January 2016, supporting business strategies:
    - Secure model approval (standard, internal, or partial) by the local regulator;
    - Develop more robust capital management and risk management capabilities;
    - Manage stakeholder interests and mitigate any issues as part of programme stakeholder management activities;
    - Maintain the confidence of the markets up to end 4Q2015 by demonstrating capability to achieve Solvency II compliance, managing stakeholders and maintaining a strong reputation for effective risk management;
    - Successfully integrate with the Solvency II implementation programme of any merger/acquired entity;

---

1   [Online]. Available at: www.towerswatson.com/ [Accessed: September 2010].

- Provide the delivery team with the support and resources necessary to deliver on objectives.

Stakeholder Communications goals and objectives
The Solvency II Stakeholder Communications strategy provides a framework for managing stakeholders and communicating programme objectives, supporting people through change and maximizing stakeholder support for Solvency II. This can be achieved as follows:

- Support the achievement of Solvency II compliance by 1 January 2016, supporting business strategies:
  - Drive stakeholder awareness, understanding, buy-in and commitment to Solvency II programme strategies and goals;
  - Drive the provision of appropriate communication and engagement channels to address the needs and requirements of different external and internal stakeholders;
  - Develop and deliver educational programmes for the programme delivery team, the Board, directly impacted staff and indirectly impacted staff;
  - Promote the image of the Solvency II programme, sharing programme wins;
  - Establish and embed streamlined and effective programme reporting process;
  - Develop and roll-out appropriate messaging to help embed a risk-management culture;
  - Provide ample communication on the nature of Solvency II, its benefits, key timelines, objectives, impacts on teams and individuals and so on, establishing dialogue via interactive forums.

When adopting any of these generic goals and objectives for a given programme, be sure to make them 'SMART' – specific, measurable, attainable, results-orientated and time-limited using internal programme plans. This will support the evaluation process where activities are assessed.

7.3 CORE PRINCIPLES

Core principles capture the essence of all Stakeholder Communications and describe key features. For example, Stakeholder Communications are:

1. Aligned to strategy – which is cascaded down via programme goals and objectives;
2. Based on stakeholder analysis, impacts and unique profiles;
3. Reflecting an equitable approach – where key constituents get more resources;

4. Reflecting a good channel mix – whereby both one-way and two-way channels are used;
5. Supportive of Solvency II programme management goals – enabling programme leaders to reach target audiences appropriately;
6. Efficient and effective – each consultation and communication activity is meaningful and relevant;
7. Supportive of change – builds awareness, understanding, compliance and commitment and focused on behavioural outcomes;
8. Supportive of culture transformation – embeds a risk culture and communicates the organization's risk appetite organization-wide;
9. Measures impact and results.

7.4 AUDIENCES AND STAKEHOLDER MANAGEMENT

Understanding our audiences is fundamental to good Stakeholder Communications. The better we know them, the better our engagement strategies and the better the overall stakeholder management process.

In Chapter 3 we saw the stakeholder map from the perspective of the EU Commission and explored the stakeholder challenge faced by the European insurance industry. Before we can even start to consider how we communicate with these stakeholders, we must first identify them using stakeholder management methodologies to ensure that all *our* stakeholders are on our radar. From there, it will be possible to appoint individual Relationship Owners who will take responsibility for managing the particular stakeholder relationship to achieve required outcomes. They, in turn can nominate direct reports as Interface Managers to take up a supporting role. In the Solvency II context, the Executive Sponsor and Programme Director are likely to manage the majority of stakeholder relationships between them, with the remainder managed by appropriate members of the senior management team. This information can be captured on a 'Stakeholder management team' chart (see Table 7.2 overleaf).

This example has been populated quite randomly purely for illustrative purposes and is customized for the UK market. For non-UK markets, the names of local regulatory bodies and lobby groups, and so on, can be substituted. Also, in this diagram, these stakeholders are grouped by nature and not by their power/interest profile (although this is indicated in the third column). For the purposes of a Stakeholder Communications strategy document, it is enough to cluster stakeholders according to their nature, as the point of this exercise is to clarify who on the leadership team is responsible for which stakeholder/s. For each category (for example, external groups) an additional group 'Other' has added so that those adopting this chart can customize it by adding their own stakeholders to the list.

Table 7.2   Stakeholder management team

No.	Stakeholder Group	Profile	Relationship Owner	Interface Manager/s
External Groups				
1	European Commission	HP/HI	Executive Sponsor	Nil
2	EIOPA	HP/HI	Executive Sponsor	Nil
3	CEA	HP/HI	Executive Sponsor	Programme Director
4	GCAE	HP/HI	Programme Director	Nil
5	PRA	HP/HI	Executive Sponsor	Programme Director
6	ABI	HP/LI	Programme Director	Programme Manager
7	CFO Forum	HP/HI	Programme Director	Programme Manager
8	CRO Forum	HP/HI	Programme Director	Programme Manager
9	Investors/ Shareholders	LP/HI	Chief Executive Officer	Executive Sponsor
10	Analysts	LP/HI	Chief Executive Officer	Executive Sponsor/ CFO
11	Ratings Agencies	LP/HI	Chief Executive Officer	Executive Sponsor/ CFO
12	Media	LP/HI	Chief Executive Officer	Executive Sponsor/ Corporate Communications
13	Tax Office	LP/HI	Tax Director	Nil
14	Policyholders	LP/HI	Corporate Communications	Programme Director
15	Recruitment Agencies	LP/LI	Programme Manager	Programme Mgt Office
16	Other			
Internal Boards and Committees				
17	Board	HP/HI	Executive Sponsor	Programme Director
18	Steering Committee	HP/HI	Executive Sponsor	Programme Director
19	BRCC	HP/HI	Executive Sponsor	Programme Director
20	Audit Committee	HP/HI	Executive Sponsor	Programme Director
21	Design Authority	HP/HI	Programme Director	Programme Manager
22	Leadership Team	HP/HI	Executive Sponsor	Programme Manager
23	Other			
Internal Groups				
24	Directly Impacted Staff	LP/HI	Programme Director	Programme Manager
25	Indirectly Impacted Staff	LP/LI	Programme Manager	Nil
26	Other			

Table 7.2   **Stakeholder management team** *(concluded)*

No.	Stakeholder Group	Profile	Relationship Owner	Interface Manager/s
	Delivery Partners			
27	Programme Team	HP/HI	Programme Director	Programme Manager
28	KPMG	LP/HI	Programme Director	CFO
29	Deloitte	LP/HI	Programme Director	CFO
30	E&Y	LP/HI	Programme Director	CFO
31	IBM	LP/HI	Programme Director	IT Director
32	Anchor consultants* e.g. Pcubed	HP/HI	Programme Director	Executive Sponsor/ Corporate Communications
33	Other			
	Other			
34	International entities	Varies	Programme Director	Varies
35	Other			

Note: * Anchor consultants are those consultants who have a big role in the implementation programme and who are critical to programme success.

This chart must be shared with any internal parties who are mentioned on it as Relationship Owners and Interface Managers so that these parties are aware of their responsibility. This will promote good practices in the business, for example ensuring that the right people in the business (senior permanent staff) are liaising with any external groups. It is recommended that Relationship Owners and Interface Managers meet as a group on a regular basis to share developments with key constituents and discuss how to manage any hot issues.[2]

7.5 KEY MESSAGES

Key messages are enduring and serve as hooks for ongoing messages which will evolve as the programme evolves. Solvency II key messages can be divided into categories, for example:

- Solvency II rational and objectives;
- Benefits for the industry;

---

2   In Dublin Airport and for the building of Terminal 2, we had a stakeholder management Steering Committee made up of executive directors who acted as Relationship Managers, reporting activity on a monthly basis and meeting as a team for peer calibration on hot issues.

- Impact on the organization;
- Impact on teams and individuals;
- Timelines;
- Programme governance;
- Messages for 'The Markets'.

Key messages will serve as core tenets for additional ongoing messaging and should be signed off by the programme Steering Committee, together with core principles and assumptions (see Section 7.8.2).

Links to company values and messages
Programme messages should also be linked to company values and messages to support message alignment. This should be apparent on externally facing channels such as websites, company reports and press releases and on internally facing channels such as the programme intranet and executive blogs.

7.6 BRANDING

A brand is used to promote the identity of its subject which may be a person, place or thing. The brand is unique to its subject, enabling different audiences to make the same or similar associations to the brand based on how it makes them feel. The more unique the brand, the more instantaneous that association will be. It may consist of a logo, slogan or name or it may simply be the use of a particular and distinctive combination of colours to represent its subject.

A brand can be a useful tool for a Solvency II programme where the delivery team is spread across geographies as it can help to unify the troops. Corporate communications may help with brand development and roll-out. However, where the delivery team is made up of different communities from newly merged entities or from different functional areas, different organizational cultures come into play. In such scenarios it may be more productive to reinforce the idea of 'one team' through key messages rather than through a programme brand. To determine the most appropriate approach, explore the idea with key stakeholders to get their input.

'Being on Brand' means being instantly recognizable across different programme communication channels, with ongoing messaging consistent. To ensure a consistent 'look and feel' use standard templates for regular communication tools such as the programme dashboard. For newsletters or other publications (online or otherwise) use the same font style and standard colour schemes. Also, as the different business leaders will generate their own messages for their own local channels, ensure the programme Steering Committee signs off key messages and core principles as these will help set a consistent tone.

7.7 CONSULTATION AND COMMUNICATIONS PLANNING

Managing stakeholders successfully will involve careful planning and the appropriate mix of communication and consultation activities.

7.7.1 Programme Stakeholder Reporting: A Central Component

During Solvency II implementation, much of the communication activity to key stakeholders will centre on reports to a host of constituencies with both shared and unique concerns.

Regular reporting allows one to achieve a number of objectives for example, keep stakeholders up-to-date, manage expectations, demonstrate organizational capability to deliver on Solvency II and establish an audit trail. On the external front, the UK financial services regulator requires a monthly report from all UK insurers and reinsurers while, on the internal front, the various Boards and Committees also require regular reports.

While it can be assumed that ever effort will be made to ensure that external stakeholders receive good quality reports and in a timely manner, when the overall reporting process has yet to be established internal stakeholders are the ones most likely to be affected leading to some of all of the following outcomes:

- Board members and Committee members receiving either not enough or too much information on the Solvency II programme;
- Board members and Committee members receiving reports from various sources that conflict with each other;
- Solvency II Programme Director having to sign off a host of reports;
- Requests for reports coming into different members of the team with multiples requests coming from different persons on the same team;
- Last minute requests for reports that were not on the radar of the Solvency II programme team.

Any one of these issues can cause a headache for the programme director. So what does a best practice reporting process look like? It includes seven key features which together negate all of the outcomes mentioned above and ensures that stakeholders receive their reports in an efficient and effective way with the minimum stress put on programme resources. The seven features are as follows:

1. Establishing one 'face of internal reporting';
2. Establish what reports are required and their audiences;
3. Map reporting requirements;
4. The central template;
5. One dashboard;

6. Scheduled updates of information;
7. The monthly reporting calendar.

One face of internal reporting
To ensure that multiple members of the team are not receiving requests for stakeholder reports, immediately appoint one person as the face of internal reporting (this may be someone in the PMO or the Stakeholder Communications Lead).

Establish requirements
Establish what reports are required and who their audiences are. It may transpire that some reports are no longer required. Also, there may be some duplication with reporting that can be eliminated. Talk to stakeholders and find out what their requirements are moving forward. Typical Solvency II reports include the following:

- External:
    - Regulator Report – monthly report for country financial regulator on programme status.
- Internal:
    - Board Report – regular update for Board members on programme status;
    - Steering Committee Pack – regular update for committee members on programme status;
    - BRCC Report – regular update for committee members on programme status;
    - Business Change Control report – monthly programme update which serves as insert for Management Information packs;
    - Risk and Compliance report – regular update for the Executive Director, Risk and Compliance;
    - Design Authority papers – papers on Solvency II design for committee members to review and base decisions on.

To get an up-to-date view of what the reporting requirements are across the business, it is worth interviewing each person who requests a report. It may transpire that some requests are being made based on outdated practices while others amount to duplication. Also, re-establish the content required for each submission to identify where synergies can be achieved with data collection.

Map reporting requirements
Based on a review of the different reports and types of information required by stakeholders develop a central template which captures all the pieces of information. Again, the following example has been populated randomly for purely illustrative purposes:

Table 7.3   Mapping reporting requirements

	Information Required	Report 1	Report 2	Report 3	Report 4	Report 5	Report 6
A	External Update	X	X				
B	Executive Summary Update		X	X	X	X	X
C	Programme RAG Status	X		X	X		
D	Summary of Key Milestones				X		
E	Key Achievements					X	
F	Detailed Milestone Plan		X	X			X
G	Financials						
H	Resources						
I	Other						
J	Other						

Such a chart serves to map stakeholder requirements and enable one to identify commonalities and differences. Once the requirement is confirmed with terminology to describe the different sections aligned, it is then possible to develop the Central Template.

The Central Template
The Central Template is a tool that can be used to update all the pieces of information required of stakeholders. Each separate piece of information is assigned a letter of the alphabet for reference purposes.

Table 7.4   The programme reporting template

The Central Template				
A. External Update	B. Executive Summary Update	C. Programme RAG Status	D. Summary of Key Milestones	E. Key Achievements
F. Detailed Milestone Plan	G. Financials	H. Resources	I. Other	J. Other

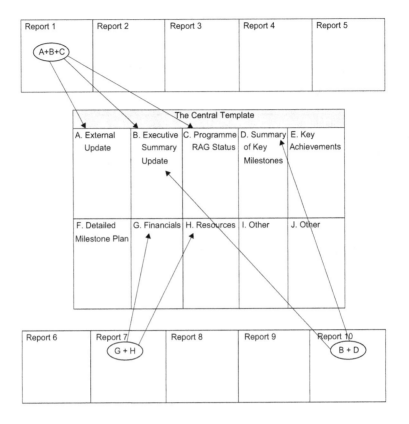

Figure 7.2   The Central Template and report population

The information stored on the Central Template can be used to populate all reports as illustrated in Figure 7.2.

One dashboard
The dashboard is a tool used by the Programme Management Office (PMO) to give a one page overview of programme status at a particular point in time. When requests for reports are dealt with independently, it can happen that different dashboards are developed based on different stakeholder information requests. If, after consideration, it is found that these requests cannot be wholly aligned, develop versions of the template which have a very similar look and feel. This benefits those senior executives who are likely to see the programme dashboard in various management information (MI) packs and saves on the confusion caused when the dashboards look different. Also, when designing a common dashboard, do ensure that Solvency II teams based in different locations and any new joiners (including merger or acquisition colleagues) are involved in the design process, so as to secure their buy-in.

Scheduled updates of information
The next thing to do is to schedule regular updates of the Central Template. These may be weekly or bi-weekly based on the needs of the organization. Updates should be scheduled after reports are in from project managers and workstream managers so that the most up-to-date information is used for programme level reports. Also, when determining the schedule, take reference from the due dates of the various reports as the shorter the time lag between a scheduled update and the submission of a particular report, the better.

◄ June	~ July 2011 ~					August ►
Sun	**Mon**	**Tue**	**Wed**	**Thu**	**Fri**	**Sat**
					1 Submit Steering Group Pack	2
3	4 Submit MI Pack SII Update	5	6 Steering Group Meeting	7 Submit Regulator report	8 Submit BRCC Pack	9
10	11	12 BRCC Meeting	13	14 Develop Change Control report	15	16
17	18 Submit Business Change report (SII Update)	19	20	21 Submit Design Authority papers	22 Submit CFO report SII Update	23
24	25	26 Design Authority papers	27	28	29 Start Board papers	30
31	Notes: Next Design Authority Meeting August 2nd, 2011 Next BRCC Meeting Sept 15th, 2011 Next Steering Group Meeting Sept 10th, 2011 Next Board Meeting Oct 10th, 2011					

Figure 7.3   Solvency II monthly reporting calendar

The reporting calendar

The reporting calendar can be set on a monthly basis and should capture the scheduled updates, when development of each different report commences, the individual report issue dates and any meetings where the reports will be discussed (see Figure 7.3). It may be created in hardcopy or online using a tool such as Microsoft Outlook™. The beauty of the online tool is that it can be used to prompt key parties involved in report development when a particular action is required of them. While this type of activity normally falls to PMO, the Stakeholder Communications Lead may wish to lead this process in the set-up stages, given how it can impact stakeholders.

Do keep in mind that while some of the reports you submit will be complete products for end users, for example the programme dashboard, others will be used as inserts to populate other reports for functions; for example, Business Change may prepare management information update reports for all projects and programmes across the business. Therefore, do track such processes so that it is clear how many times in a month a particular stakeholder (such as a senior executive) will be updated on Solvency II developments. Also, work with those who are using inserts to compile their own reports, to ensure that updates are not amended in any way.

Finally, if it is the case that a there is a significant time lag between a report being submitted to the Board and that report being reviewed at a Board meeting, do ensure that the person presenting the report has the most up-to-date brief and can share any new developments. Figure 7.3 is an example monthly calendar using Win Calendar™.

7.7.2 Strategic Consultation Plans

When a programme is host to large number of stakeholders and when Relationship Owners have been identified, it is useful to develop a Strategic Consultation Plan for each stakeholder. This plan will provide a one page summary of the stakeholders' profile, key contacts, strategic issues and objectives, planned interventions, the consultation and communication channel mix of activities plus timelines. There should be little changed to the content over time, although change is not ruled out. Chapter 8 focuses on the development of plans.

7.7.3 External Communications

External communications activity is typically managed centrally by a Corporate Communications function. Typical external communication channels include press releases, interim and annual reports, presentations and question and answer sessions for the analysts and investors and press briefings. The strategy document can establish how Corporate Communications and Stakeholder Communications interact, naming key parties and roles. For example, Corporate Communications will own the various channels with the Solvency II programme owning the messages to stakeholders on Solvency II. The Solvency II Stakeholder Communications workstream will act as a 'one-stop shop' for Solvency II messaging, while their Corporate Communications colleagues will act as an enabler, helping to get the messages to external stakeholders using the right channels and in a timely and appropriate way. For such cooperation, activity alignment and message alignment will be key issues to manage, particularly where a parent body exists and inputs into the process.

7.7.4 Internal Communications

Internal communications activity is also typically managed centrally and often stands alone but, alternatively, it may sit in Corporate Communications or even in Human Resources. Internal communications will own organization-wide communications, a key stakeholder group being the workforce as a whole. Channels can include the main internal magazine and other publications, the company intranet and other online forums, executive blogs, events, competitions and employee engagement surveys. Again, the Stakeholder Communications workstream will act as their one-stop shop for Solvency II messaging, with their Internal Communications counterparts acting as an enabler, helping to get the messages to stakeholders in a timely and appropriate way using the right channels. The strategy document should clarify on such points to make transparent how the touchpoint functions successfully. To ensure message alignment and activity alignment, messages and plans should be shared on a regular basis. The Solvency II programme may indeed develop its own internal communication channels such as dedicated intranet pages, an executive blog and a team newsletter.

Given that 50 per cent of Solvency II programmes are being driven from back office functions there is likely to be one more key communications touchpoint and this is likely to be the local Finance or Risk Communications Manager. Their universe will be their particular functional area. The Stakeholder Communications Lead will provide them with Solvency II related messaging while they will act as an enabler, sharing functional communication channels. Where a Centre of Excellence (COE) approach has been adopted for Internal Communications, the network will act as business partners and enablers for the business and there will be clarity of roles and responsibilities. Where the COE approach does not exist, lack of clarity may exist around roles and responsibilities and this could serve as an obstacle to getting things done. Developing a plan to get clarity on such issues will require smooth operations (see Appendix 2).

7.7.5 Training and Development

Induction training
As newcomers to the Solvency II team come on-board, they need to be brought up to speed on the new regime and internal programme status. A customized induction

programme can meet their needs and this may be delivered once a month by the subject matter experts.

Newcomers to the larger organization also require induction material on Solvency II. This may be incorporated into a large HR induction programme for all newcomers to the organization, and it may be followed up with brief but mandatory CBT training module on Solvency II. The latter can serve to verify that all staff have a certain level of awareness and understanding of Solvency II.

Solvency II Board training
The EU Directive is explicit in its high expectation of Board involvement in Solvency II and this responsibility cannot be delegated. In fact, the regulators will be interviewing Board members on their understanding of the organization's risk framework and how the risk appetite is reflected in decision-making processes, as part of the process for assessing whether a firm is compliant or not. Therefore, the pressure is on for Board members to get 'up to speed'. This is where Solvency II Board training comes in.

Key Board training topics recommended by Rory O'Connor of EMB[3] include (programme) implementation plans, risk appetite and business strategy, the risk management system, the Internal Model and internal and external disclosures (this would include new metrics for M.I.). Other topics can include the responsibilities of the Board under Solvency II, the overall training approach and director requirements, assumptions and methodology, the ORSA process, the 'use test', the 'culture test' and the Solvency II balance sheet. This content can be used as the basis to create a core programme schedule with modules positioned to coincide which the Board's BAU activity where possible. This approach introduces a practical element to the training and helps Board members make connections. Also, where possible, use real examples of the company's risk management framework, and so on, to make the learning experience practical and meaningful. With many non-executive directors concerned that they are increasingly being expected to be no different from executive directors, using straight-forward language and real examples will help secure their buy-in for learning experience. The most effective programmes will follows these top ten best practices:

1. Explicit alignment between learning objectives and business objectives;
2. Positive cost/benefit ratio with measurement techniques indicating clear return on investment either in the shorter term or longer term;
3. Learning relevant and useful, and timed with business as usual activity to make it easily transferrable back to the workplace;
4. Learning aligned with and directly supported by organizational structure, values, performance management, and so on;

---

3   www.emb.com.uk/.

5. Multiple methods used to drive home learning; block training supported by 1–1 sessions, role-plays, mock interviews, and so on;
6. Content uses real examples and plain language to support the learning experience;
7. Training programme strategy development led by training expert in line with best practices;
8. Training delivered by subject matter experts and expert facilitators; the use of consultants for delivery allow for a strong external view on how internal practices compare with industry peers and when trainers have expert facilitation skills, this encourages open discussion and avoids a lecture approach;
9. Board members encouraged to develop their own self-directed training, based on their learning experiences with other Boards they sit on and other industry exposure;
10. Board meetings encourage a work habit of ongoing reflection and learning based on the new Solvency II requirements and their everyday duties.

Training for directly impacted staff
Training for those who use capital in their decision-making should centre on helping them to understand model outputs and how to interpret and use data, and also the risk culture philosophy and how it applies to them. Those impacted by organizational change should also be provided with training on how to manage change successfully. Face to face training is recommended so that people can ask questions to get clarity, and seek guidance.

Training for indirectly impacted staff
Those who do not use capital in their day-to-day business will be impacted by the implementation of Solvency II alongside BAU activities and the embedding of a risk culture. Programmes for these staff, such as a mandatory computer-based training (CBT) module, will focus on developing a certain level of understanding. Participant rates and results for such a module can provide a useful audit trail that demonstrates that the risk appetite and culture is being communicated across the organization.

A programme of Solvency II Business Briefings can be developed and rolled out on a priority basis with 'high power, high interest' stakeholders being first on the list to receive such a briefing. The material can be based on a core set of content introducing the Solvency II regime, latest timeline, and so on, with additional content added to address unique stakeholder issues. As with the Solvency II Board training programme, these briefings can be delivered by subject matter experts, with the Stakeholder Communications workstream developing the plan, coordinating materials development and driving successful roll-out.

Table 7.5   The Stakeholder Communications risk log

No.	Risk	Likelihood	Impact	Result	Mitigation
1	Key stakeholders not onboard in terms of Stakeholder Communications strategy and messaging.	H	M–H	Communications suffer in terms of appropriateness of messages and channels and the timeliness of message delivery damaging stakeholders' perception of the Solvency II programme.	Circulate strategy to Steering Committee and secure sign-off at the appropriate level.
2	Board members fail to convince the Regulator that the organizations risk appetite has been communicated widely, internally.	H	H	Undermines Regulator perception and rating of the organization in terms of Solvency II compliance.	Deliver communications and training to the Board to enhance understanding of Solvency II, and support communication of organizations risk appetite widely and internally.
3	Board members fail to convince the Regulator that they understand Solvency II related issues as they should.	H	H	Undermines Regulator perception and rating of the organization in terms of Solvency II compliance.	Deliver regular reports and Solvency II training to the Board to enhance understanding of Solvency II.
4	Key stakeholders receive poor information on Solvency II programme status (e.g. lack of info, conflicting info, out-of-date info, too much info to digest).	H	H	Key stakeholders make wrong decisions that affect strategic direction of Solvency II programme based on poor information.\n\nCredibility of Solvency II programme management is undermined.	Establish and embed streamlined reporting process that ensures key stakeholders get external updates and programme reports efficiently and effectively.
5	Stakeholder Communications (effectively 'People Change') workstream marginalized by technically focused programme management.	H	H	Lack of resources and support lead to a firefighting approach with little proper oversight or governance processes.	Scope work, establish workstream where none formally exists, allocate appropriate resources, provide support and steer, include progress in monthly reports and programme dashboard and apply governance processes.

#	Risk			Consequence	Mitigation
6	Communications fail to engage in-directly impacted internal stakeholder groups appropriately.	M	L–M	Required behavioural outcomes for key audiences not be achieved – for example with low levels of awareness amongst key audiences (e.g. directly impacted staff) a risk management culture could not be embedded.	Messages to stakeholders are based on identified stakeholder impacts and requirements (of Solvency II environment) and defined behavioural outcomes for each group using the 'Buy-in Escalator' (Ref. p. 63).
7	Communications fail to engage external stakeholder groups appropriately.	L–M	H	External stakeholders e.g. 'The Markets' lack confidence in capability of organization to implement Solvency II successfully and achieve compliance status.	Roll-out timely and effective Solvency II external communications plan based on stakeholder requirements and with Solvency II Steering Committee/ Executive Sponsor sign-off.
8	Communications not involved in debate around 'what is communicated' as well as 'how it is communicated'.	H	M	Key messages could fail to be delivered. Impact of these messages on audience would not be foreseen/ understood. Programme could face serious resistance.	Solvency II Stakeholder Communications Lead to attend meetings and all forums where 'what is being communicated' is agreed.
9	Senior Stakeholders disseminate Solvency II messages via their own communication channels without consulting the Stakeholder Communications Lead.	M	M	Lack of co-ordination in communications leading to lack of alignment in terms of activities and lack of alignment on messaging. Credibility of the Solvency II programme would be undermined.	All Solvency II messaging to go to Solvency II Stakeholder Communications Lead for programme level approval prior to disseminat on.
10	Messages conflict across various businesses (where multiple businesses exist).	M	M	Solvency II communications would not support the delivery of communications objectives in different parts of the business.	Stakeholder Communications Lead responsible for ensuring all Solvency II messages are aligned and intervenes where inconsistencies arise.

7.8 THE RAID LOG

Programmes and projects are made up of structured and interdependent activities that are organized to facilitate effective change. Those activities are refined down to a level of detail that can be effectively managed, defining who does what and when. If all went according to such plans, programme and project management would be quite a straightforward endeavour. However, even the best plans go wrong due to unforeseen events. In fact the reason programmes and projects often go over schedule is not because they are badly planned, but because of those unforeseen events that were not planned for. Managing such events can quite easily double the amount of time required to deliver to schedule.

RAID is a project management acronym that stands for Risks-Assumptions-Issues-Dependencies. The RAID log supplements the traditional programme or project plan. It helps help to manage the overall workload by taking into consideration risks, assumptions, issues and dependencies which can be logging on a spreadsheet, with one tab devoted for each of these four items. The RAID log should be regularly reviewed and updated in conjunction with the main plan.

7.8.1 'R' for Risks

Risks are a classic component of programme and project management. Risks are potential events that could happen and lead to delays, additional costs and deteriorated quality. Risks are managed by identifying and putting into action mitigating actions that reduce the likelihood of either the risk happening or, should the risk occur, of its impact. A risk log will include a description of each risk, an indicator of the likelihood of each risk occurring, an indicator of the level of impact should a particular risk occur and a description of the mitigating actions that need to take place to decrease the likelihood of the risk occurring (and thereby its impact). Risk logs can be supplemented by supporting detail that indicates before-and-after mitigation assessments and risk owners. A Stakeholder Communications risk log would look something like that shown in Table 7.5.

7.8.2 'A' for Assumptions

Assumption management is the systematic identification, analysis, planning and review of assumptions to ensure they remain appropriate (reasonable) and consistent.[4] To focus assumption management, the plan or decision frames the context and assumptions are generally reserved for cases where a change in

---

4   Project and programme management, Introduction to assumption management, Ministry of Defence, www.aof.mod.uk [Accessed: November 2010].

assumption would have a material bearing on the plan or decision. Often in the programme and project management context a disparate group of delivery partners are brought together to deliver on plans. Each is working in accordance with his/her own culture and experiences and unconscious assumptions. Therefore, when planning a new programme or project, it is worth capturing those unconscious assumptions that relate to fundamental principles about how work is organized and, for example, where the boundaries of roles are. Captured assumptions may then be agreed by key stakeholders, for example, the Solvency II Programme Steering Committee, and deliberately tested in the workplace.

The assumption log will include the assumption itself, and may also include the rationale for why this is assumed and the action to be taken to confirm or otherwise that the assumption is or is not valid. Assumptions that underpin how Stakeholder Communications operates may include some or all of the following:

- Solvency II Stakeholder Communications owned by the Solvency II Stakeholder Communications workstream which liaises with interested parties at various touchpoints across the organization;
- Solvency II key messages and assumptions are shared with relevant parties who communicate on Solvency II to ensure message alignment;
- Solvency II Stakeholder Communications worksteam develops content for internal communications;
- Solvency II Stakeholder Communications workstream develops content for external communications;
- Final drafts of any Solvency II messaging is submitted to the Solvency II Stakeholder Communications Lead for approval at programme level (programme lead or executive sponsor), before dissemination into the public domain.

Governing principles and assumptions articulate a set of foundational concepts that underpin policies, practices and processes. They should be validated with key stakeholders.

7.8.3 'I' for Issues

Issues are risks that have materialized and the issues log is where they are captured and tracked. If the risk planning activity has been conducted properly, any issues that do in fact materialize will not be a surprise and post-event contingency actions will be identified for auctioning where possible.

The issues log will include a description of each issue, the actual effect it is having (as opposed to the expected effect) and the actions that must be taken to mitigate and remove the issue.

Table 7.6   Stakeholder Communications dependencies

No.	The Dependencies Log
1	Given the appropriate level of authority to deliver on responsibilities and accountabilities.
2	Stakeholder Communications Strategy signed off by key stakeholders.
3	Briefed and kept up-to-date on Solvency II programme progress and any developments.
4	Invited to key meetings where decisions are made that will impact Stakeholder Communications.
5	Invited to key operational meetings to agree communications within Solvency II programme team.
6	Provided with clear and consistent messages and an appropriate steer.
7	Provided with adequate resources to support delivery.
8	Provided with ample notice to produce and distribute Solvency II communications.
9	Given sign-off on Solvency II messaging and materials in a timely manner so as to facilitate timely dissemination.
10	Given oversight of any final Solvency II messages prior to dissemination.

7.8.4 'D' for Dependencies or Decisions

Programme and project management is not unlike normal BAU activity in that there is a service chain of internal and sometimes external customers who depend on us and who we in turn depend on to deliver. Although an individual may be working well and in line with their own schedule, they may experience a set-back when someone whom they rely on fails to deliver in time or to the required quality. Often this happens because those people whom we depend on have other priorities; what is urgent to us is not as urgent to them.

The dependencies log can help management such situations by capturing, at a minimum, whom we are dependent on, how we are dependent on them, plus what they should deliver to us and when. The log may also capture details of any agreement and when such agreements were made, plus any later variations of these.

To be positioned to deliver, the Solvency II Stakeholder Communications workstream will have specific requirements, or dependencies, that must be met. Firstly, and as with any communications role, one must be provided with input to create output; the Stakeholder Communications Lead cannot exist in a vacuum and must be kept informed of developments as they occur, and involved in key meetings. Other dependencies centre on more operational issues that enable timely and effective communications. All key dependencies are listed in the table opposite. When these dependencies are met, the Stakeholder Communications Lead will be best positioned to deliver.

Sometimes on a RAID log, 'D' may be taken to mean 'Decisions' in addition to, or instead of 'Dependencies'. In project and programmes, decisions are sometimes made that can have a significant effect on delivery, but that impact has been poorly thought through. Decisions made along the way can create extra work, impose extra costs, and lead to confusion and frustration for those left to manage the knock on effects.

The decision log will capture, at a minimum, the decision made, its rationale, the name of the decision-maker and the details of any resulting work required. This process helps to ensure that decisions made along the way do not destabilize the plan. It also provides a useful point of reference when the questions are asked 'Why did we decide to do that?' and 'Who made the decision?'

7.9 RESOURCING

7.9.1 Budget

The budget for Stakeholder Communications will be determined by the overall approach taken. For example, if a low-profile approach is planned, the budget will be low. However, where a high-profile strategy is adopted, costs may be significantly higher. Also, the strategic stakeholder management planning piece is not likely to incur additional costs; rather, the majority of costs will be incurred on the delivery side of the plan and on items such as Solvency II Board training, CBT programmes and internal communications vehicles.

Consider, for example, the costs of running an in-house town-hall-type meeting. One would be forgiven for assuming that there are no costs involved, but in fact costs could include:

- Hiring of staff event hall for main event:
  - Fee to Social Club for use of room;
  - Fee to Facilities management for room set-up and tidy-up;
  - Fee to hire equipment such as microphones and audio-video equipment.
- Social event that follows:
  - Drinks;
  - Finger food/sit down meal.
- Post event:
  - Fee for development of short video recording of event.

Other items that are likely to incur costs include off-site meetings, training materials and CBT programmes, quality publications such as booklets and support materials for roadshows.

7.9.2 Manpower

For a large programme, this workstream will consist of a workstream lead, a communications/events person, a learning and development manager and an administrative assistant. Alternatively, and for a small programme, it may consist of one individual who works with various parties across the organization to implement the strategy, with strong logistical support from the PMO. The level of resources allocated should reflect the size of the programme plus the scope and size of the workload.

Typically, the Stakeholder Management Lead will advise the Programme Director and s/he may be a member of the programme Steering Committee. Key touchpoints across the organization will include company secretariat (for Board communications), corporate communications (for external Stakeholder Communications), internal communications (to reach staff), human resources (to align with messaging and activities with the HR agenda), learning and development (for learning materials development), business leaders (to meet the requirements of impacted staff), corporate strategy (for culture and change issues) and business change control (to input into reports for the leadership team which cover all projects and programmes across the organization). His/her focus will be on planning, and tracking process against plans, while leading the team on the delivery piece.

7.10 KEY MEASURES

The goal in the evaluation section is to lay out how to measure success on two levels – activity and results.

7.10.1 Results

At the end of the programme implementation, a review should be conducted to establish if objectives were achieved. Ideally, it will be possible to compare results achieved to business results and identify where change management activities would have had a direct impact. During implementation, such reviews should be held periodically. Ultimately, measures of success will include evidence of strong stakeholder buy-in, both internally and externally, and the ability of the Board to convince the Regulator that they have a sound understanding of Solvency II, are making risk-based decisions and have embedded a risk culture across the organization.

7.10.2 Activity

As the stakeholder engagement plan will involve a staged roll-out of communications and training activity, it is possible to track activity over time, using quantitative and qualitative measures and progress against plans. Take for example if quarterly Solvency II Board training is being held. Successful activity would include smooth logistics and elements of the project plan being implemented in a timely and effective way, with positive participant feedback and behavioural change. Reviewing such activity has the added benefit of allowing one to take corrective action if activities aren't getting the desired results.

Based on programme milestones, choose suitable points at which to measure the success of activities and their impact. Depending on the nature of activities on the plan, other potential metrics can include:

- Media coverage:
    - How much coverage did the Solvency II related story receive?
    - What was the tone of the coverage?
    - Which media channels was the coverage in? Where was it positioned in those channels? What is the audience of that channel?
    - Were programme key messages used?
    - Was the company spokespeople quoted?
- Company intranet Solvency II forum:
    - How many visitors were there to the forum during a particular time period?
    - How long did they spend in the forum?
    - Which pages did they visit?
    - Did they download material? Is so, what material?
    - Did they raise questions and leave feedback?
- Stakeholder buy-in to proposals:
    - How did different stakeholders react?
    - Are they responding as expected?
    - Is their buy-in increasing or decreasing?
    - What percentage of their issues and concerns has been mitigated?
    - Overall, what percentage of stakeholders are supportive compared to day one of engagement plan rollout?

These are just a few examples of metrics. The metrics for a particular Stakeholder Communications plan will depend on the scope of the activities. Feedback can be solicited via surveys, interviews and focus groups.

7.11 CHAPTER SUMMARY

A Solvency II Stakeholder Communications strategy is a document which can be used by management to outline the planned approach to maximize programme stakeholder support and meet agreed goals. It can also serve to illustrate how programme management networks and interacts with audiences – a process which is iterative and evolving in nature. The strategy will have a cross-functional impact with its reach extending to external stakeholders. Key features of the strategy design include an introduction, an outline of principles, goals and objectives, audiences and stakeholder management, key messages, branding, consultation and communications planning, programme stakeholder reporting, the RAID log (risks, assumptions, issues and dependencies), resourcing and key measures.

CHAPTER 8

COMMUNICATION PLANS

Stakeholder Communications is all about getting the right messages to the right constituents in a timely and effective manner so as to develop understanding and resolve issues with a view to securing compliance and, ultimately, buy-in. As outlined in the previous chapter, it will involve the development of strategic consultation plans to cater for the needs of specific clusters of stakeholders, an internal communications plan to reach across the whole organization, and an external communications plan to reach across external stakeholder groups.

8.1 STRATEGIC CONSULTATION PLANS

Strategic consultation plans provide an overview of the issues of a particular stakeholder plus the strategies and interventions planned to manage the relationship. A typical strategic consultation plan will include:

- The name of the stakeholder group;
- The profile of the group (for example, HP/HI = 'high power/high interest');
- The overall strategy for dealing with the stakeholder (for example, 'manage closely');
- Members of the group plus the representative appointed to liaise with programme management;
- The appointed Relationship Owner and Interface Manager;
- Strategic interests and objectives of the group;
- Programme management interventions and communication channels;
- Overall completion date.

8.1.1 A Strategic, Localized Approach

Strategic Consultation Plans are owned by the appointed Relationship Owners, though the Stakeholder Communications Lead can help with plan development. They are a useful reference point for Steering Group discussions on how to engage with a particular stakeholder that is proving challenging. Also, and as the name suggests, they are meant to be strategic. Any such plan should fit onto one A4 page and provide a clear overview of key points for a person who is not familiar with the stakeholder or with the context. Strategic consultation plans serve as a useful frame of reference for programme Steering Committee discussions on how to proceed with a particular stakeholder. Busy executives have a lot of material to read and digest, so keep the Strategic Consultation Plan simple so that it acts as an aid and not an impediment to communication.

8.1.2 A Tactical, Centralized Approach

Where one individual is responsible for managing the majority of stakeholders an alternative approach is to capture, on an Excel spreadsheet, all information available on all stakeholders so as to provide an overview of all activity. The first sheet can focus on those with 'high power, high stake' profiles, the second on those with 'high power, low interest' profiles, the third on those with 'low power, high stake' profiles and the fourth on those with 'low power, low interest' profiles. On each of these sheets, or pages, stakeholders can be listed down the page vertically, with those headings listed in the bullet points in 8.1 captured across the top, horizontally. As there is no space limitation, other headings can be added; for example, date of next event due, a (Red, Amber, Green) RAG status can be added to each stakeholder to facilitate a rough temperature check of the relationship in terms of their awareness, understanding, buy-in and commitment to programme objectives and/or a column can be added to track where else activity is captured, for example monthly reporting calendar, internal communications plan or external communications plan. In fact when this plan is fully developed it may render the internal and external communications plans obsolete. Given the scope of this engagement plan, populating it should be a team effort and not left to one individual. Measurement activities should be carried out on two levels – activity and results. Activity can be tracked via hard facts, for example number of meetings, briefings, bilateral held per month. Measures for results will vary and may be based on an assessment by the Relationship Manager as to how cooperative and/ or happy the stakeholder is with developments on the programme, whether or not an internal stakeholder signed off on key decisions, whether or not an external stakeholder publicly endorsed the direction of the programme, and so on.

Apart from providing a helicopter view of all activity, this approach has other advantages:

- By focusing on any particular stakeholder, it becomes clear to the less informed that stakeholder engagement is achieved via a variety of channels with the core of the activity being bilaterals, group meetings and (for important stakeholders) regular social activities such as evening meals; this is quite different to an 'internal communications plan' which focuses largely on employee engagement.

Table 8.1 Solvency II Strategic Consultation Plan for the Board

		Solvency II Stakeholder Group – The Board				
Profile	Strategy	Members and Rep.	Owners	Issues and Objectives	Interventions	Key dates
HP/HI	Manage Closely	Sir David O'Brien (Chair) Adam Nelson		Oversee successful implementation of Solvency II in the business in line with EU Directive requirements and in line with peers	Participation of Board representatives in programme Steering Committee meetings	Up to point where organization secures Solvency II compliance status (before 1 January 2016)
		William Scott Michael Hopkins	Relationship Owner – CEO, Jonathan Daniels	Be able to demonstrate to regulator risk-based decision-making in line with Solvency II requirement, understanding of risks faced by business and risk appetite	Board agenda and decision-making linked to Solvency II themes	Ongoing
		Dame Juliette Harper Daniel Reidy (NED)	Interface Managers – CRO, Sue Coleman and Solvency II Programme Director Adam Hill		Structured Solvency II Board Training sessions followed by mock interviews, records of risk-based decision-making in Board meeting minutes	Quarterly sessions over 2014 and 2015
		Harrison Culligan (NED)		Embed risk culture and ensure communication across organization of organization's risk appetite and how it affects business	Ensure alignment of organization's risk culture with Solvency II and the communication of both across the organization	Ongoing
		Eamonn O'Donovan (NED) Board Representative		Mitigation of Solvency II related Board issues/ individual Board member issues	Board meetings, bilateral meetings and social events with Executive Sponsor and programme management	Ongoing

- Where resources are tight on the Stakeholder Communications workstream, this plan makes it abundantly clear where resources must be focused – on facilitating those interventions that will support engagement with 'high power, high interest' stakeholders (for example, Solvency II Board training, Solvency II business briefings, Solvency II Induction training for team members and townhall type events for Solvency II team members which allow face to face interaction with programme management). While having a Solvency II team newsletter is a 'nice to have', for example, it is not going to make or break successful implementation programme, but it could divert resources from the needs of 'high power, high interest' stakeholders.

8.2 INTERNAL COMMUNICATIONS PLAN

Internal communication serves as the glue that links the different parts of the business together. Much of the communication is informal and carried out on a one-to-one or small group basis. But there is also a requirement for strategic cross-functional communication that engages the broader workforce and aligns all with common goals and objectives. Such communications are more formal and will be carried out by an Internal Communications function.

A Solvency II internal communications plan will capture formal cross-functional communications that have a Solvency II focus and address programme stakeholder needs. As mentioned in the previous chapter, and where a particular communication channel is owned by Internal Communications, the Stakeholder Communications workstream will provide and approve Solvency II stories and messages. Some channels, though, such as the programme director blog and programme team newsletters, will be owned by the Stakeholder Communications workstream.

Before developing an internal communications plan it is good practice to take stock of the current situation. An audit will determine if employees are receiving information of the Solvency II programme and progress, if the information is accurate, if messages are consistent across the company and how interested employees are in Solvency II. As outlined in Chapter 7, useful information can be gleaned from:

- Organization goals and objectives;
- Solvency II programme goals and objectives;
- Visits to key branches;
- Surveys to gather stakeholder input;
- Focus groups;
- Desk research;

- Interviews with key stakeholders;
- Discussions with colleagues;
- Observation of everyday practices.

Such output may have been collected and consolidated as part of the strategy design exercises, unless it is clear that there has been little done yet to engage in enterprise-wide communications of Solvency II. In such a case, it would be the wrong use of resources to conduct in-depth background research.

To develop an internal communications plan you need to know who the audiences are, the communication goals and objectives, what the over-arching key messages are, which channels are appropriate, who will own the implementation of the various communication activities and appropriate roll-out dates.

8.2.1 Audiences/Stakeholders

Appropriate audience selection is critical to the success of the internal communications plan. Imprecise audience selection leads to an unfocused, ineffective roll-out of communications while well-defined audiences help the crafting of communications that help achieve objectives. As established earlier, all Solvency II internal stakeholders can be clustered into four groups:

- Governance;
- Committee;
- Directly Impacted Staff;
- Indirectly Impacted Staff.

Communication and consultation activity with those stakeholders who fall into the 'Governance' and 'Committee' clusters will be informed by the relevant Strategic Consultation Plans and will mainly focus on group meetings, bilateral and social activity. This means that the main target audiences for the programme-level Internal Communications Plan are Directly Impacted Staff and Indirectly Impacted Staff (where the Tactical and Localized approach is taken as outlined in 8.1.2, Directly Impacted Staff may be already covered).

Know your audiences. If you know one audience is going to have concerns about a certain aspect of Solvency II, make sure the messages for them specifically address that issue. Likewise, if they're looking for reassurance about a particular point and it is possible to give that reassurance, then do so. And make sure people have channels for giving feedback. Taking stakeholder concerns into consideration will help minimize resistance and secure support. Also, think about where each stakeholder group stands on Solvency II. In they are very opposed it will be a big challenge to secure compliance and buy-in. If they are not interested, they may get annoyed with what they perceive as too much communication on Solvency II.

Table 8.2   Solvency II key messages: internal

Solvency II Rationale and Objectives	• To align capital requirements with the underlying risks of an insurance company; • To maintain strong, effective policyholder protection while achieving capital allocation; • To develop a proportionate, risk-based approach to supervision with appropriate treatment both for small companies and large cross-border groups; • To provide incentives to insurers to adopt more sophisticated risk monitoring and risk management tools – this would include developing full and partial internal capital models and increased use of risk mitigation and risk transfer tools; • To achieve a harmonized approach to supervision across all EU markets – this will help to ensure there is a level playing field for all insurers and should provide a common standard of protection to all consumers regardless of the insurers' legal form, size or location; • To increase competition within EU insurance markets and the global competitiveness of EU insurers – reducing or removing unnecessary regulatory constraints and adopting a coherent 'lead supervisor' approach for pan-European Groups. This will provide more choice and a better deal for EU consumers, and also enable EU insurers to compete more effectively in global insurance markets, in line with the Lisbon agenda.*
Benefits for the Industry	As per section 1.1.2 of this book, Solvency II is expected to reap the following benefits: • More protection for policyholders; • Reduced risk of market disruption; • Better risk-based capital assessment through the use of Internal Models and better integration of risk and capital management; • Improved enterprise risk management and governance; • A more informed and assured basis for decision-making; • Industry homogeneity and alignment.
Timelines	• EU Directive finalized – 2009; • March–December 2012; • Omnibus II – 20 January 2011; • Level 2 Delegated Acts finalized March/April 2012; • Level 3 Guidance finalized July 2012; • 'Go Live' date for Solvency II – 1 January 2016.
Solvency II Issues	• Standard formula may make some firms appear financially less secure (not necessarily capturing unique risk profile of a given firm); • Costs of implementation of Solvency II and the Internal Model; • Some parts of the Solvency II framework are considered overly prudent, for example, 'Allowance of Liquidity Premium' and the rate of the 'Cost of Capital'; • If the new solvency regime results in more capital becoming encumbered, the rate of emergence of cash flow will becomes less certain for both the debt holders and shareholders.

Benefits for the Organization	**Governance:** • Improves oversight and active mitigation of risks. **Capital Management:** • Ensures Capital works harder promoting customer confidence. **Risk Management:** • Financial risk now managed alongside operational risk; • Focus on risk-based capital and abolition of multiple regimes of capital reporting will lead to greater transparency of the real risks faced by the business and the link between risk and capital; • Reduces the operational costs of reporting on multiple capital bases. **Common Language:** • Provides a common language for discussion on risk and capital (for example, 'risk culture' and 'risk appetite'). **Alignment:** • Bring actuarial, risk, compliance and audit personnel closer together in their day-to-day work practices, aligning goals and objectives.
Solvency II Programme Goals and Objectives	The objectives of the Solvency II implementation programme are to: • Secure model approval (standard, internal, or partial) by the local Regulator; • Develop more robust capital management and risk management capabilities; • Manage stakeholder interests and mitigate any issues as part of Solvency II programme stakeholder management activities; • Maintain the confidence of the markets from 2Q2010 to 4Q2012 by demonstrate capability to achieve Solvency II compliance, managing stakeholders and maintaining a strong reputation for effective risk management; • Successfully integrate with the Solvency II implementation programme of any merger/acquired entity.
Programme Governance	Governance structure: • Our programme Executive Sponsor is (add job title and name of individual); • Our Steering Committee is chaired by (add job title and name of individual who may be the Executive Sponsor or CRO); • Our Steering Committee is the implementation programme governing authority and links in with various Committees and the programme Design Authority (share with programme organization chart).
Messages for Teams and Individuals	• Everyone in the organization will be impacted by Solvency II, some more than others; • Impacts have been mapped per stakeholder groups and this information has informed tailored communications for each group; • For 1Q – 2Q2011 we will be focusing on those who will be impacted the greatest; • For directly impacted staff, we are ensuring the support is there to ensure that people know what is expected of them in the Solvency II world; • For indirectly impacted staff, we are ensuring that all appreciate what Solvency II is and what it means for our organization.

Note: * Solvency II – Understanding the process, Feb 2007. [Online]. Available at: www.cea.eu/ [Accessed: August 2010].

8.2.2 Communication Goals and Objectives

The communication goals and objectives articled in the strategy document will inform the communications plan (as will the core communication principles); for example:

- Drive the provision of appropriate communications to address the needs and requirements of different internal stakeholders;
- Support the embedding of a risk culture;
- Support the workforce through change.

8.2.3 Key Messages

Over-arching key messages inform all communications that will be developed. They help to ensure that message consistency and make sure the programme is communicating the right things to the right people. The messages will permeate all communications and will attract the attention of decision-makers so it is important that due care is given to their development. Below, key messages are crafted for the key message categories mentioned in the previous chapter. These over-arching messages will remain constant while other messages will evolve as Solvency II evolves.

8.2.4 Channels

An extensive inventory of communication channels was provided as a resource in Chapter 4. This included booklets and computer based training for all staff on the organizations risk culture and risk appetite and how these link to individual performance and measurement, the intranet, executive blogs, off-site events and newsletters, and so on. Be sure to adopt a mixture of information channels and engagement channels for each stakeholder group to achieve the desired impact and support the achievement of the required behavioural outcomes.

8.2.5 Activity Owners

For each communications activity, owners will be assigned and given responsibility for implementation. This section may be sub-divided to indicate who develops the communications, who signs off on it and who is responsible for dissemination.

8.2.6 Roll-Out Dates

Selecting appropriate roll-out dates for different communication activities will involve taking a step back to consider the big picture and what other activities are going on around the business. Getting a clear view with require a conversation with the owner of the cross-business internal communications plan. It is important to know what is going on and when so that activities do not clash. For example, if a team social is being planned then it should not clash with any other activities which demand the attendance of team members because such a clash could result in non-attendance, a negative impact on team morale and costs that cannot be recouped. Also, selecting appropriate roll-out dates will require a look into executive diaries and calendars to know who is where and when. If a particular executive is a key speaker at a team event, check their availability before confirming the date of the event and booking team diaries.

When all such information has been collated it can be used to populate the Internal Communications Plan template like the one in Table 8.3 which gives an overview of activity for the month. Such an action plan is very useful to planning resources and organizing the workload. A higher level plan can also be developed which gives the overview of communication activities for a quarterly, half-yearly or annual period.

Remember, effective internal communications is a means to an end, and not an end in itself. Keep that thought uppermost when developing the plan.

8.3 EXTERNAL COMMUNICATIONS PLAN

According to the research findings shared in Chapter 2, insurers and reinsurers implementing Solvency II have been internally focused, with little engagement with external stakeholders. This needs to change to maintain market confidence.

Table 8.3   Internal Communications Plan template

October 2014					
Audience	Outcome Required	Key Messages	Channel	Owner	Date

8.3.1 Audiences/Stakeholders

The Solvency II External Communications Plan outputs will be targeted at the following stakeholder groups:

- The Markets – investors, analysts and ratings agencies;
- SIGs – media[1] (commentators, trade media and the city) and policyholders.

Other external groups that take an interest in programme external communications may include:

- Lobby groups – for example, CEA, GCAE, CEO Forum, CRO Forum;
- Regulators – local and European (for example, PRA (UK) and EIOPA);
- The competition/industry peers.

8.3.2 Communication Goals and Objectives

External communication goals and objectives should be concerned with:

- Reinforce brand, conveying strong solvency and capital position and optimization:
  - Affirming market confidence that the organization can successfully implement Solvency II;
  - Sharing key programme achievements;
  - Sharing the benefits of Solvency II for investors and demonstrating how Solvency II adds value to the business;
  - Providing the markets with updates on programme progress to raise their comfort level and increase confidence;
  - Clearly conveying risk management;
  - Clearly communicating any significant change to risk appetite that will affect product return;
  - Mitigating issues and concerns;
  - Highlighting key issues of concern during the consultation process; for example, in the UK 'illiquidity premium' developments are the current hot topic.

---

1   If bloggers are to be included, find out who has an interest in Solvency II and who is likely to be receptive to the organizations key messages. And be careful – while it is standard practice to disseminate press releases indiscriminately to the media network, this approach is not a wise one to take with bloggers. They are far more likely to go online and publicly complain if they don't like what they hear. So do your homework first – identify their interests, what their views are and whether it is a good idea to include them at all.

8.3.3 Key Messages

In addition to the key messages shared in Section 8.2 (such as 'benefits for the organization', 'programme goals and objectives', and 'key achievements'), a separate set of key messages are required for The Markets. In particular, it is important to outline the benefits of Solvency II for investors and to make sure the markets are initially comfortable and then confident that the organization can deliver.

Table 8.4   Solvency II benefits for markets and investors

Messages for the Markets	• We are using the (Standard/Internal/Partial) model to calculate SCR. • We are engaging with the Regulators on the journey towards gaining (Internal/Partial) model approval. • Our engagement with the Regulator is going to plan. • Evolving regulation could impact contingency plans but don't expect the direction of travel to change. • Contingency plans are in place if we do not secure Internal/Partial model approval. • We have adequate capital in place while securing IMAP (as appropriate). • Going through the IMAP process requires rationalization of end to end reporting process due to timescales required for disclosure (as appropriate). • Our view on a particular key issue under consultation is (share view).
Benefits for Investors	• Increased disclosure on governance and integration of risk and capital management is likely to promote increased discipline. • Economic capital and regulatory capital will be better aligned, meaning investors and regulators will have the same worldview (traditional FSA returns did not have much information content for investors). • Better aligned market valuations for assets and liabilities from the perspective of both regulators and investors. • Greater ERM discipline. • Short form of the SFCR report which is seen by many as too cumbersome in fuller form.

Messages may be incorporated into year end report topics such as:

- Introduction to Solvency II – aimed at policyholders, to clearly articulate what Solvency II is and forthcoming developments.
- The benefits and impacts of Solvency II – aimed at policyholders, to clearly articulate how Solvency II will benefit different key constituents and how it will impact the organization.
- Solvency II programme goals and objectives – the plan plus progress against plan.
- Solvency II programme key achievements – share wins to strengthen confidence.
- Solvency II activity and engagement update – discussion on lobbying activity.
- Changes in governance and risk management as a result of Solvency II – headline changes and reasons for changes (material changes to be disclosed in the SFCR once live).
- Solvency II risk culture embedding in the organization/group – headline steps taken to align risk culture with Solvency II requirement.
- Impact on capital – share quality of capital compared to the Solvency I regime.

Start with sharing generic programme information and, over time, increase the level of disclosure on Solvency II related activity. Also, monitor and review on an ongoing basis competitor disclosures on Solvency II. It may be that the organization chooses to work with industry peers to craft additional shared messages relating to issues under consultation that are causing concern for the industry, for example illiquidity premium in the UK. The target of such messaging will be the Regulators who will be also monitoring industry disclosures on Solvency II and the objective will be to positively impact the final outcome.

8.3.4 Channels

External communication channels include:

- Press releases;
- Interim and annual reports and statements;
- Presentations and Q&A sessions for analysts and investors;
- Lobbying activity reports.

For any external Q&A sessions, anticipate questions and prepare responses developing a Q&A document for internal reference only. This process will be driven by the Stakeholder Communications Lead who will collate the answers from the appropriate subject matter experts for the review of the programme director and possibly the Steering Committee also. This Q&A will act as a briefing sheet for those taking the questions – usually the CEO and the Head of Corporate Communications. Typical questions include:

- What progress are you making implementing Solvency II?
- What are the programme key milestones and deliverables for 2014/2015?
- How will Solvency II impact your Balance Sheet?
- What is the effect of the key issue (name issue) on your business?
- How will Solvency II impact the product strategy?
- How will it impact the Group (as appropriate)?
- How will the 'use test' change how things are done?
- How will Solvency II change the culture?
- Are you bankrupt?

8.3.5 Activity Owners

With external communications, it is not only good practice but imperative that stories and messages are signed off internally before they are released into the public domain. Once the Stakeholder Communications Lead has drafted messages and they are reviewed, revised and approved by the programme director they must be signed off. This sign-off process may go through the Solvency II programme Executive Sponsor or Steering Committee, or it may go through Corporate Communications/Investor Relations and the CEO. Owners of the various channels will be responsible for roll-out.

8.3.6 Roll-Out Dates

Key financial dates for the year will inform the external communication plan and which channels are to be used. Below is the financial calendar of Prudential Financial Inc:

- Q1 2011 Prudential Financial, Inc. Earnings Release Wednesday 4 May 2011 *Q1 2011 Prudential Financial, Inc. Earnings Conference Call* Thursday 5 May 2011 11.00 a.m. ET.
- *Prudential Financial Inc Annual Meeting of Shareholders* Tuesday 10 May 2011 2.00 p.m. ET.
- Prudential Financial, Inc. 2011 New York Investor Day Thursday 9 June 2011.
- Q2 2011 Prudential Financial, Inc. Earnings Release Wednesday 3 August 2011.
- Q2 2011 Prudential Financial, Inc. Earnings Conference Call Thursday 4 August 2011 11.00 a.m. ET.
- Q3 2011 Prudential Financial, Inc. Earnings Release Wednesday 2 November 2011.
- Q3 2011 Prudential Financial, Inc. Earnings Conference Call Thursday 3 November 2011 11.00 a.m. ET.

When developing the external communications plan, it is important to remember what lasting impression stakeholders should take away with them after communication activities events. Is it one of comfort or confidence that the organization can successfully implement Solvency II? Perhaps it is both – first develop a degree of stakeholder comfort and progress to developing confidence. On the Solvency II journey, there has been so much uncertainty in the market about the timeline and what implementation means for the business that developing external stakeholder comfort with programme developments and achievements would be a good start towards securing buy-in.

8.4 CHAPTER SUMMARY

Stakeholder Communications is all about getting the right messages to the right constituents in a timely and effective manner to get the manage issues and achieve the desired impact. It can be best achieved through the use of a mixture of strategic consultation plans, which cater for particular groups, an internal communications plan which targets indirectly impacted staff, and possibly directly impacted staff also and an external communications plan which caters for the needs of constituents such as investors, analysts, policyholders and the various sections of the media. While the industry research found that Solvency II affected entities were largely internally focused and engagement (with external engagement limited to regulators and lobby groups and for the purposes of internal implementation), the time has come for a holistic approach that extends to all key parties. Only by securing the confidence of key stakeholders, internally and externally, can the interests of the organization be best served.

APPENDICES

APPENDIX 1

The CEA is the European insurance and reinsurance federation. Through its 33 member bodies – the national insurance associations – the CEA represents all types of insurance and reinsurance undertakings, for example pan-European companies, monoliners, mutuals and SMEs.

1. Austria – Verband der Versicherungsunternehmen Österreichs (VVO), www.wo.at
2. Belgium – Assuralia, www.assuralia.be
3. Bulgaria – Асоциация на Българските застрахователи, www.abz.bg
4. Croatia – Hrvatski ured za osiguranje, www.huo.hr
5. Cyprus – ΣΥΝΔΕΣΜΟΣ ΑΣΦΑΛΙΣΤΙΚΩΝ ΕΤΑΙΡΕΙΩΝ ΚΥΠΡΟΥ, www.iac.org.cy
6. Czech Republic – Česká asociace pojišťoven, www.cap.cz
7. Denmark – Forsikring & Pension (F&P), www.forsikringogpension.dk
8. Estonia – Eesti Kindlustusseltside Liit, www.eksl.ee
9. Finland – Finanssialan Keskusliitto, www.fkl.fi
10. France – Fédération Française des Sociétés d'Assurance (FFSA), www.ffsa.fr
11. Germany – Gesamtverband der Deutschen Versicherungswirtschaft (GDV), www.gdv.de
12. Greece – ΕΝΩΣΗ ΑΣΦΑΛΙΣΤΙΚΩΝ ΕΤΑΙΡΙΩΝ ΕΛΛΑΔΟΣ, www.eaee.gr
13. Hungary – Magyar Bistosítók Szövetsége (Mabisz), www.mabisz.hu
14. Iceland – Samtok Fjármálafyrirtækja (SFF), www.sff.is
15. Ireland – The Irish Insurance Federation (IIF), www.iif.ie
16. Italy – Associazione Nazionale fra le Imprese Assicuratrici (Ania), www.ania.it
17. Latvia – Latvijas Apdrošinataju Asociacija, www.laa.lv
18. Liechtenstein – Liechtensteinischer Versicherungsverband e.V, www.versicherungsverband.li

19. Lithuania – Lietuvos draudiku asociacija, www.draudikai.lt
20. Luxembourg – Association des Compagnies d'Assurances du Grand-Duché de Luxembourg (ACA), www.aca.lu
21. Malta – Malta Insurance Association, www.maltainsurance.org
22. Netherlands – Verbond van Verzekeraars in Nederland (VVN), www.verzekeraars.nl
23. Norway – Finansnæringens Fellesorganizasjon (FNO), www.fno.no
24. Poland – Polska Izba Ubezpieczen (PIU), www.piu.org.pl
25. Portugal – Associaçao Portuguesa de Seguradores, www.apseguradores.pt
26. Romania – Uniunea Nationala a Societatilor de Asigurare si Reasigurare din Romania (UNSAR), www.unsar.ro
27. Slovakia – Slovenská asociácia poistovni, www.slaspo.sk
28. Slovenia – Slovensko Zavarovalno Zdruzenje (SZZ), www.zav-zdruzenje.si
29. Spain – Unión Española de Entidades Aseguradoras y Reaseguradoras (Unespa), www.unespa.es
30. Sweden – Sveriges Försäkringsförbund, www.insurancesweden.se
31. Switzerland – Schweizerischer Versicherungsverband, www.sw.ch
32. Turkey – Türkiye Sigorta ve Reasürans Sirketleri Birligi, www.tsrsb.org.tr
33. United Kingdom – Association of British Insurers (ABI); International Underwriting Association of London (IUA); Lloyd's, www.abi.org.uk

Source: www.cea.eu/ [Accessed: 2 May 2011].

APPENDIX 2

Clear roles and responsibilities for programme Stakeholder Communications and functional communications roles can create synergies, especially where a 'Centre of Excellence' approach to Internal Communications has yet to be established.

Table A.1   Stakeholder Communications roles and responsibilities

	Role (Internal Comms Element)	Primary Audience	Governance
SII Stakeholder Communications for strategic programme that has organization-wide impact	Creating and delivering strategic and tactical internal communications to support the SII programme meet internal and external stakeholder needs	Programme 'High Power, High Impact' Stakeholders For centralized approach to stakeholder management, work down to 'Low Power, Low Impact' stakeholders based on resources available	SII Programme Director SII Steering Committee
Internal Communications team for e.g. Risk division	Creating and delivering strategic and tactical communications to support e.g. the Risk division	Risk community	Risk Manager

Table A.1   Stakeholder Communications roles and responsibilities *(continued)*

	'Universe'	Specific Examples	Touchpoints
SII Stakeholder Communications for strategic programme that has organization-wide impact	Organization-wide and external	Reports and packs for meetings with external stakeholders Customized SII business briefings for directly impacted teams and indirectly impacted teams Events, roadshows, publications, blogs, conferences and workshops	SII activities that involve the risk community (e.g. SII focus groups for risk) Risk activities that impact SII activities (e.g. certain meetings)
Internal Communications team for e.g. Risk division	Risk function and ad-hoc organization-wide	Events, roadshows, publications, blogs, conferences and workshops	

Table A.1   **Stakeholder Communications roles and responsibilities** *(concluded)*

Emergent Issues, Risks	Mitigation
Boundaries of roles Boundaries of roles need to be clarified Lack of clear boundaries will lead to confusion and impact teamwork	**Boundaries of roles** Get clarity on roles and boundaries and agree on processes that support good boundaries and get sign-off from those who oversee both roles
Activity alignment Both roles needs to be aware of activities on either side Lack of alignment will lead to confusion, activities clashing and impact teamwork	**Activity alignment** Monthly calendars of activities created and shared upfront
Message alignment SII messages need to go through SII Stakeholder Communications Lead. Risk messages need to go through Risk Communications Manager. Lack of alignment can lead to inappropriate messaging that can damage perceptions of the programme and of the value of work being carried out by team	**Message alignment** Share key messages Ideal intervention is to establish Centre of Excellence approach to Internal Communications across the organization so as to nullify emergent issues and risks

BIBLIOGRAPHY

BOOKS

Argis, C., 1993, *Knowledge for Action. A Guide to Overcoming Barriers to Organizational Change*, Jossey-Bass, San Francisco.

Bower, M., 1966, *The Will to Manage*, McGraw-Hill.

Buckham, D., Wahl, J. and Rose, S., 2010, *Executives Guide to Solvency II*, Wiley, USA.

Eden, C. and Akerman, F., 1998, *Making Strategy, The Journey of Strategic Management*, Sage Publications.

Johnson, G. and Scholes, K. (eds), 2001, *Exploring Public Strategy*, Pearson Education, Harlow, UK.

Mendelow, A., 1991, *Proceedings of the 2nd International Conference on Information Systems*, Cambridge, MA.

O'Donovan, G., 2006, *The Corporate Culture Handbook*, The Liffey Press, Ireland.

Prosci Inc., Creasey, T. and Hiatt, J., 2012, *Best Practices in Change Management: 575 Organizations Share Lessons and Best Practices in Change Management*, Prosci benchmarking report, Loveland, USA.

Schein, E., 1992, *Organisational Culture and Leadership*, 2nd Edition, Jossey-Bass, USA, p. 231.

JOURNAL ARTICLES

Bryson, J., Cunningham, G. and Lokkesmoe, K., 2002, What to Do When Stakeholders Matter: The Case of Problem Formulation for the African American Men Project of Hennepin Country Minnesota, *Public Administration Review*, 62:5, 568–84.

Freeman, R.E. and Reed, D.L., 1983, Stockholders and Stakeholders: A New Perspective on Stakeholder Governance, *California Management Review*, 25:3, 83–94.

Mitchell, R.K., Agle, B.R. and Wood, D.J., 1997, Towards a Theory of Stakeholder Identification and Salience: Defining the Principle of the Who and What Really Counts, *Academy of Management Review*, 22:4, October, 53–886.

O'Donovan, G., 2003, Change Management: A Board Culture of Corporate Governance, *Corporate Governance International*, 6:3, September.

ONLINE

Accenture, 2010. Available at: www.accenture.com/ [Accessed: December 2010].

Banana Skins survey, Centre for Financial Services Innovation in association with PricewaterhouseCoopers, 2007. Available at: www.pwc.com/ [Accessed: April 2011].

BestWeek Europe, 2010. Available at: www.ambest.com/sales/BestWeek/ [Accessed: December 2010].

Countdown to Solvency II, PriceWaterhouse Coopers, 2007. Available at: www.pwc.com/ [Accessed: September 2010].

Delivering Solvency II, Issue 1, Financial Services Authority, UK, 2010. Available at: www.fsa.gov.uk/ [Accessed: September 2010].

Edwards, T., Solvency II Challenges Facing the Insurance Market, 2010. Available at: https://ktn/innovateuk.org/ [Accessed: February 2011].

European Insurance – Key Facts, CEA, 2010. Available at: www.cea.eu/ [Accessed: September 2010].

European Insurance – Key Facts, Insurance Europe, 2013. Available at: www.insuranceeurope.eu [Accessed: January 2014].

Getting Ready for Solvency II, PricewaterhouseCoopers, Fig. 2, p. 12, 2010. Available at: www.pwc.com/ [Accessed: December 2010].

Getting Set for Solvency II, PricewaterhouseCoopers, 2010. Available at: www.pwc.com/ [Accessed: December 2010].

Lessons Learnt from the Crisis: Solvency II and Beyond, CEIOPS, 2009. Available at: www.eiopa.eu/ [Accessed: December 2010].

Media release following 'ICAS 2007 and the Path to Solvency II', 2007. Available at: www.abi.co.uk/ [Accessed: April 2011].

Ministry of Defence, Project and Programme Management, Introduction to Assumption Management. Available at: www.aof.mod.uk [Accessed: November 2010].

Moody's Analytics, 2013. Solvency II Practitioners' Survey: A Field of Missed Opportunities?, Exhibit 9, p. 10. Available at: http://www.moodysanalytics.com/2013solvencyiisurvey [Accessed: January 2014].

Outlook, Ernst and Young, 2010. Available at: www.ernstandyoung.com/ [Accessed: November 2010].

Solvency II Bulletin, vol. 19, Association of British Insurers, UK, 2010. Available at: www.abi.co.uk/ [Accessed: January 2014].

Solvency II Overview, Scandinavian Capital Solutions, 2010. Available at: www.scandanaviancs.com/ [Accessed: February 2011].

Solvency II – Understanding the Process, CEA, 2007. Available at: www.cea.eu/ [Accessed: September 2010].

The Same but Different, Deloitte, 2007. Available at: www.deloitte.com/ [Accessed: November 2010].

Tiwari, A., CEO, Aptivaa Consulting, Solvency II, 2008. Available at: www.aptivaa.com/ [Accessed: November 2011].

Why Excessive Capital Requirements Harm Consumers, Insurers and the Economy, CEA, Brussels, 2010. Available at: www.cea.eu/ [Accessed: November 2010].

Ziewer, L. and Wyman, O., 2009. Adapted from 'Assess the Business Impact of Solvency II' [Accessed: December 2010].

INDEX

Page numbers in **bold** refer to tables; page numbers in *italic* refer to figures; page numbers followed by 'n' refer to notes at the bottom of the page.

Printed in the United States
by Baker & Taylor Publisher Services